Dear Jiles,

This is the second effort. I did not think that I was going to write another book and then this happened. Thank you for your simple, yet very appreciated support!

I Love you!

Praise for
The Wounded Healer

"*The Wounded Healer* squarely addresses the elephant in the room: How do I escape the pain I've lived with my whole life? The answer turns out to be both unexpected and paradoxical.

"The author provides us the answer with every chapter. I found myself rooting for each of the people whose pain is shared as each chapter comes alive with the human experience. And this is what's behind my binge reading . . . 'Can they see the truth? Will they have the courage to do so?'

"This is an amazing read and EXACTLY what I needed and hoped for."

Kelley McCabe, Founder of eMindful

"*The Wounded Healer* will inevitably spark a deep and unusual inner journey in anyone aspiring to become more conscious and compassionate. It may not have been Chaleff's intention when writing it, but his book leaves a lasting effect."

Peter Koenig, Author and Inventor of *The Money Work*

"Andy is a present-day astronaut, except his space is the deep, dark reaches of the mind, and he brings the flashlight of truth and a healthy dose of self-love for oxygen."

Phyllis Serene, Author of *All My Heroes Were Ho's*

"*The Wounded Healer* is a book that shares love, pain, suffering, and hope through Andy's interactions with others. He is not afraid to be vulnerable as a human or as a writer, which implores the reader to stay engaged and to explore his or her most inner terrain."

Lemuel W. Watson, Associate Vice President for Diversity, Equity and Multicultural Affairs at Indiana University

"Andy's insights are like curveballs. Counter-intuitive (or maybe counter-culture), the things you can learn from his story offer a type of freedom often found by doing and realizing the exact opposite of what we thought we knew."

Josh Whiton, Founder of TransLoc and MakeSoil

"I started to thumb through *The Wounded Healer* and it brought me to tears. A lot. I must've cried thirty different times reading it, and eventually got through the whole thing in a day. It really helped me get in touch with my grief. It was just sitting at the surface waiting to get out. Thank you for this book!"

Jeff Liebermann, Host of Discovery Channel's *Time Warp*

"Andy fearlessly engages with a diverse cast of characters struggling to fit into an increasingly confusing world. Along the way, sparks fly, tears are shed, and even a little pee is unintentionally released. Reading the book is a wonderful experience, and Andy's insights are very helpful for me to better understand my own relationships and how I interrelate with loved ones."

Gino Yu, Associate Professor Hong Kong Polytechnic University

"The transparency with which Andy writes is as clear as his way of living: present and deeply attuned to his surroundings and the people he encounters. Reading *The Wounded Healer* is a chance to meet Andy in person on every page; and to meet Andy is to fall in love with the richness and fullness of life. This one book I keep picking up and rereading segments to remind me of what it is like to be fully present."

Kris Girrell, Author of *Wrestling the Angel*

The Wounded Healer:
A Journey in Radical Self-Love

by Andy Chaleff

© Copyright 2020 Andy Chaleff

ISBN 978-1-64663-121-6

Published by

köehlerbooks™

210 60th Street
Virginia Beach, VA 23451
800–435–4811
www.koehlerbooks.com

THE WOUNDED HEALER

A JOURNEY IN RADICAL SELF-LOVE

ANDY CHALEFF

VIRGINIA BEACH
CAPE CHARLES

TABLE OF CONTENTS

The Guest House

Rumi

This being human is a guest house.
Every morning a new arrival.

A joy, a meanness,
some momentary awareness comes
as an unexpected visitor.

Welcome and entertain them all!
Even if they're a crowd of sorrows,
who violently sweep your house
empty of its furniture,
still treat each guest honorably.
He may be clearing you out
for some new delight.

Be grateful for whoever comes,
because each has been sent
as a guide from beyond.

Welcome

"We are all just walking each other home."
−Ram Dass

Look in the mirror and say, "I love you." Seriously. Try it. Look into your own eyes and say, "I love you."

If you're like most people, you'll find it at least uncomfortable, if not impossible. We're constantly finding things not to love about ourselves. The things that have been quietly eating away at us. Our weaknesses and mistakes. Our embarrassments and failures. Our disappointments and frustrations.

I've struggled to love myself all my life. But in 2017, I decided to do something about it. I didn't know how to fully love myself, but I resolved to push the limits of my comfort zone. I would no longer allow self-doubt to dictate my decisions and limit my potential. I would no longer conveniently step sideways when facing a challenge. I would no longer allow feelings of vulnerability to close me off.

It all began the day after my wedding, June 12, 2017. In the trough that often comes after big events, I decided to write a book. I was not a writer, nor did I have a clear theme. But there would be a book—of that I was certain. I decided to let my instinct guide me.

While on my honeymoon, I awoke each morning at five a.m. Under the covers next to my wife, Rani, I wrote what turned into hundreds of pages on my iPhone. I relived every meaningful moment in my life, paying special attention to the ones filled with shame, guilt, and pain. The writing turned into its own healing process as I exposed—and ultimately learned to accept—the parts of me that were hiding in the shadows.

This all culminated in a book, *The Last Letter: Embracing Pain to Create a Meaningful Life*. To my surprise, the book was well received—so well received that I felt like I had a dilemma on my hands. If I was to fully embrace the success of the book, then I'd need to overcome my first hurdle: embracing the spotlight. In order to do that, I felt it would need to be ambitious. Something that pushed me out of my comfort zone.

While showering one day, the idea hit me. I decided to travel across the US for three months and ask people one simple question: *If you knew someone in your life would die tomorrow and you had one last chance to express feelings to him or her, what would you say?* It was the very question I posed at the end of *The Last Letter*.

Over time, my general idea became more focused and concrete, and I outlined a basic structure for my trip. I planned to travel from the west coast to the east, with the goal of hosting sixty "Last Letter" sessions. In each session, I would share my own story of pain described in my book, and then invite participants to write their own "last letter" to the person of their choosing. These could be letters of love, gratitude, forgiveness—any emotion people felt compelled to express that would give them greater healing, peace, and freedom.

I mapped my route based on people whom I knew throughout the US. I asked friends and connections if they would host these Last Letter sessions. As people agreed, my route unfolded. I then located bookstores along my route and cold-called them to see if they would host sessions as well. To my surprise, many of them readily agreed. My trip was set.

This book is the story of that journey. Throughout the journey, I hope you'll find themes that resonate with your life. Challenging experiences you have had trouble putting behind you. Old patterns you wish you could eliminate, but that still control your life. Experiences of shame and guilt. Moments when you have found it hard to accept and love yourself. And last but not least, the internal voice that says you're not good enough, that beats you up for all your past mistakes.

Although I have enjoyed relative success, the disapproving voice of my father has always haunted me: "Andy, you'll never amount to anything." It has prevented me from fully accepting and loving myself. It has often made me pull back and bunt instead of letting go and swinging for the fences.

We all have our own voices. The voices of critical parents, teachers, friends. The emotional baggage from the past that weighs on us. The shame and guilt we try to stifle. The accumulation of all our life struggles. I spent most of my life trying to manage all these psychological and emotional burdens in myself. It took me decades to realize I had been getting it wrong all along. Instead of moving away from it, I should have been running directly into it. Like a beautiful waterfall that may sting for an instant, but then massages.

In my classes for clients, I'm often asked, "How do I get rid of these voices, these thoughts, these emotions?"

My answer is almost always the same: "What if you didn't need to get rid of them, but instead, loved them? How do you love that thought so much that it's no longer unconsciously wreaking havoc in your life? What if it didn't need to be resolved, but instead completely embraced?"

It's instinctual for us to label thoughts as "positive" or "negative." In this mindset, we embrace the positive and resist the negative. This leads to a trap. Once we judge thoughts as negative and believe they're bad, we are defined by our desire to resist them. The moment we resist a negative thought, it controls us. In this space, we can never find peace—because we'll never run out of "negative" thoughts to plague us.

Alternatively, we can see that thoughts are just that: thoughts. They are immaterial connections spinning around in our heads, nothing more. The challenge we all face is, how can we slow down and analyze the instinctive process of attaching judgments of good or bad to thoughts? How can we become less defined and limited by the thoughts that we resist?

For me, there are no negative thoughts. There are just thoughts—ideas that pop into my head and take me away from my direct experience of this moment. At times, I attach value judgments (i.e. good and bad) to them. When I do that, they begin to define me in the world. To the degree that those judgments go unseen, I react to those thoughts. It's in those moments that I get lost, frustrated, confused, lonely.

Because this is the core challenge people face when they feel stuck emotionally, you'll see this process in action throughout this book. It will make more sense as you read real-life examples.

Allowing thoughts to be, just as they are, with no judgments of them, allows us to reflect on them more freely. When we can see that some thoughts create unpleasant emotions, we can ask, *What is it about this thought that gives me this feeling?*

Here is where radical self-love comes in. Instead of trying to solve the thought, we see what happens when we embrace it at the root. We no longer resist it or try to make it go away.

Although I have taught this countless times, I still have areas in my own life that I don't love completely. On this trip, I resolved to change that. I promised myself I would push my limits and look where it was hardest to look, to love what was the hardest to love in myself. *intention.*

You're now part of this journey. My travel companion. Join me as I discover how finding radical self-love radically changed my experience in the world. At the same time, I'll share with you the simple practice I use to support others to do the same. I offer my journey as a possible doorway to your own discovery of self-love.

In the journey to radical self-love, we learn how to heal from our deepest emotional triggers. We learn to accept all the things we wish we could change about ourselves. We fully embrace the things we resist—and even celebrate them. By doing so, we release the stranglehold they have over us.

Throughout this journey, I travel to meet with old friends and family, spiritual communities, the leaders of Silicon Valley. I even drop in on retirement homes and a group of psychics. As I learn how to give my own emotions a place, the people I meet along the way begin to freely explore their own—especially the hard ones, the ones associated with people who have hurt us.

With the help of a simple exercise I use along the way, the pattern of self-judgment is interrupted and subdued. The brain isn't allowed to fall back into the critical mode that keeps it stuck: the nagging, "would have, could have, should have" thoughts about everything we wish we could take back, or everything we wish we would have done before it was too late.

Paradoxically, it is in accepting our helplessness, incapacities, and imperfections that we find liberation. And it all begins with radical self-love. Welcome to the journey.

CHAPTER 1

Surrendering at the Airport

(Amsterdam, The Netherlands)

September 1, 2018. Six a.m. I get up to leave for the airport. I bring with me a few meaningful objects as a way of staying grounded and connected throughout my trip. One of these objects is my uncle's watch, which I received after he passed away. It gives me the sense that I am not alone.

I'm nervous. My friend Raoul drives me to the airport. Rani considered seeing me off at the airport, but we agreed to say goodbye at the house. It is hard enough to leave her for three months. I have done my best to plan everything, but I arrive at the airport and notice that the watch is not on my wrist. I have a moment of sadness, and then laughter sets in. I realize that whatever comfort I expected the watch to bring me, it is time to let that idea go with the rest of my comfort zone. Like a sweet message from the universe saying, *Andy, this is your journey.*

I see in the moment that I can either fall prey to the lost expectation or surrender to the new reality. I have learned throughout my life that letting go of my own expectations is a far more healing and rewarding path.

I walk to the front desk to check my baggage and am met by Geert, a KLM Airlines attendant. He doesn't meet me with an inviting smile, but rather a blank statement: "Your ticket, please." I take out my phone with the details and hand it over with my passport. He looks at both for a long time and I begin to worry. *Did I confuse the date of the flight?*

He then looks up at me as a doctor might, to give bad news to a patient, and says, "Your names don't match. Your passport says 'Andrew' and your ticket says 'Andy.'"

I am confused. I say, "I have never had a problem with this before."

He picks up the phone to call a supervisor, who instructs me to visit the service center. "You will not be able to board the flight with this ticket," he says.

I insist, "Yes, but I have flown the same flight three times this year and I've always used the name Andy."

My arguments go nowhere. I laugh because I realize that if I am going to survive the three months ahead of me, I will need to have more patience. I must surrender to whatever materializes in front of me. Now I need to surrender to what feels like one of the most absurd things I could imagine: my identity.

I know full well that along this journey I will need to let go of much of my identity. The things that I dearly want may not always be possible. If I am going to survive sixty sessions, then I cannot force anything. I will need to accept what shows up, regardless.

The beautiful irony, of course, is that this journey is a grand experiment in allowing my identity to dissolve into the background. To feel at peace with whatever I might be expected to be. Yet the first challenge I'm confronted with is the need to prove my identity.

I take my ticket and passport to the service desk, where it is explained that up to three letters can be different from the passport and the ticket, which was my case. I am told that the agent wasn't aware of this.

I laugh for the third time and realize that if I am going to survive these three months, I'll need to be prepared to deal with a lot more adversity than just a mix-up with my name. It will be a time to find peace in the storm. Whatever that storm might be.

CHAPTER 2

Screwing it All Up

(Seattle, Washington)

I arrive in Seattle from Amsterdam and drive to my friend Steve's house. Steve and I were college roommates. We had an interesting relationship because, unbeknownst to me at the time, Steve was in love with me. He bought me gifts all the time. Being naïve, I always equated that with him just being very nice.

A few years after graduating from college, I was living in Vienna and received a letter from Steve. He shared his deep regret that he had not told me he was gay and had been in love with me for all those years. He also shared that he revealed this to his parents and they asked him to seek counseling from their church to fix the "problem." In his letter, he asked me if I could forgive him.

I responded to Steve and wrote, "The only thing I am angry about is that you have not yet accepted who you are and fully embraced it. You are a gay man with nothing to hide. Nothing to fix. Nothing to heal. The fact that your parents aren't able to accept this yet is not your issue. They will figure it out in time. Now it's time for you to stop hiding yourself! I love you even more."

I wanted Steve to feel full of love and acceptance of the thing causing him so much anxiety and fear of rejection.

Throughout the years, Steve and I continued to stay in touch. I met his husband and their daughter. Coming back to stay with Steve is emotional. We reminisce about our time away. About the craziness of being college kids and the pain of not being able to accept ourselves for who we were.

Steve and I also have a special bond because he dropped me off at the airport the first time I left the US almost thirty years earlier. There, at LAX, we had a good cry. As he explained to me later, my leaving was one of the hardest moments of his life. I was somehow the one person that he could rely on at that time, and now he was alone. Thirty years ago, Steve dropped me off at the airport when I was running away from my pain. Now, my journey to accept and love my pain begins with him.

My first session is this evening, at a spiritual bookstore called East West. It is one of the many locations that I emailed with my proposal. I'm nervous, so I arrive more than an hour earlier than scheduled. I have no idea what to expect.

As I walk into the bookstore, the first thing I notice is a large poster with my face on it. The thought that my face is on anything is just weird to me. I stare at it for a few moments, taking it in. Of course, this is the natural consequence of all of the energy that I put into this project, but it is surreal. I feel fear rise up in me as I think to myself, *Seeing that poster, people are going to have expectations.* I am greeted by the store manager, who asks me for a stack of books to place at the register, then guides me to a back room where the session will take place.

There is a stage with a microphone and a podium with a Tibetan cloth draped in front. I walk in and say, "We certainly will not be needing that. I'll be sitting in a circle in the middle of the room."

I set up, and then walk around the bookstore. There are tarot cards and all sorts of minerals—everything you'd expect to find in a spiritual wellness store, including lots of incense.

I place five chairs in a circle, thinking it will be better to plan for fewer and add more if required. A few minutes later, people begin to arrive. To be specific, three people. Admittedly, on one level I am relieved. I have a testing ground to work with. I pull the circle in tighter and do what feels most intuitive.

Two of them are women who appear to be in their forties, and are the types you'd expect to see at a spiritual bookstore. Both are wearing crystals around their necks and one is wearing a tie-dye shirt. These two are warm and open. They greet me with a hug, as if we've known each other for years. The third woman is a therapist, who greets me with a handshake.

After sharing my reason for the trip, I share my childhood story, going back to the death of my mom. I hear myself say, "My mom was killed by a drunk driver." I notice it for a few reasons. The first is that I realize I could also say, "She died in a car accident." But for some reason that feels so far removed from what happened. The story I created all those years ago was that she was killed. Taken away from me without notice.

As I hear the word "killed," it feels quite aggressive. I have desensitized myself to it. The next thing that I notice is that I swallow the emotion. I have a tendency to hold my pain in my throat and I notice a tightness form when the words come from my mouth. At the same time, I see how quickly I jump over it. It has become a story and no longer my experience.

As soon as I notice this, I slow down my speech and say, "I'd like to repeat that. My mother was killed by a drunk driver." This time I feel the tears. I have made the resolution that I am not going to step over the pain. This is the first moment I hold myself to that resolution. I cry.

I haven't been aware for all these years that I've hidden behind these words until this very moment. It is as if I have trained myself to turn off my brain's emotional center while I say it, if only to function in the world. I am quite certain that it is a requirement for my emotional survival, but at this moment I want to do more than just survive. So I cry. I can see that the group is able to make space for my tears and I am not uncomfortable that they witness this.

After sharing my story, it's time for the letter-writing portion of the session. I pass out the paper and pens I've brought and explain the exercise to them. *If you had to write a last letter to someone, who would it be to, and what would you say?* It's an exercise in emotional release and connection. I give them thirty minutes to write their letter.

I decide at this moment to write a letter of my own at each session. If I am asking others to do so, then I'll need to lead by example. I also decide that I will read to the group whatever I write, no matter how challenging it is.

As we come back into the circle, I realize that having people read their letters is going to be confronting. I certainly don't want people to feel forced into that level of vulnerability. I start by saying, "Please share whom you wrote to and why you wrote them."

The first to speak is the therapist. She shares that she wrote a letter to her daughter. She says, "My daughter had a baby recently and she has refused to let me see her or the baby."

We all sit quietly and she continues. "My sisters are very angry at her and I feel sorry for her that they are angry."

As she speaks I feel an immense amount of anger and frustration from her. We all do. It is palpable. She continues to speak about her daughter, ignoring her own emotions.

As I listen I have a bright idea. *Andy, why not experiment? Why not take some risks and see if you might be able to inspire some real change?*

I decide to share with her the tool I use for finding self-acceptance. I learned the tool from my friend, Peter Koenig, who is an expert at helping people raise their consciousness in their relationship with money. He calls his tool "projections and reclamations work." He invites people to first identify their mental projections of money, and then twist them. For example, a person might project onto money the belief, "Money is security." In that case, Peter would invite him to say, "I am insecure without money, and that's okay."

In this process, people dissolve their unconscious projections so that fewer and fewer aspects of their lives are driven by unconscious beliefs. In short, when you bring your unconscious beliefs into the light and then accept them as they are, they lose their power over you. As Carl Jung said, "Until we make the unconscious conscious, it will drive our lives and we will call it fate."

I've learned to use this same practice with everything I resist in myself. I dig deep until I find the thing that hurts the most to say out loud. For example, when I feel helpless in a situation I can say, "I am helpless, and it's okay." I apply it to situations where I have experienced pain from other people. "My father never accepted me, and it's okay." I also apply it to my own shortcomings and mistakes. "I'm selfish and it's okay."

Over the years, I've used this tool consistently to accept uncomfortable or painful experiences, deeply-rooted beliefs, things I dislike about myself. In this way, I find peace without needing to change or fix anything. If I learn to completely accept something I'm resisting, it's no longer a problem. And when it's not a problem, it holds no power over me. I can simply observe experiences, thoughts, and feelings without reacting to them.

This is in contrast to the perspective I often see in the personal development world, which is to find those deeply-rooted beliefs and then try to change them. In my experience, this process actually creates more resistance, and therefore more confusion and pain in oneself. I have found that absolute acceptance is the easiest, most effective way to change anything in myself—although, ironically, my intention is not to change anything at all.

So while sitting in this first session with this angry woman, I think, *Why not give it a try?* With reckless abandon, I say, "I'd like to try something. Could you say, 'My daughter is being a real bitch, and it's okay.' In doing this, I break several rules. I do not ask for permission. I do not meet her in her pain. I do not even show recognition that I realize how difficult it will be to repeat those words.

That's when it goes to shit. She says, "Why are you judging my daughter?"

I reply, "I am not judging your daughter. I don't know her."

She continues, "Yes, you are judging her. I see it. You're judging her."

I do my best to recover. "First, let me apologize. I tried something that obviously didn't work and I am very sorry for that."

She interjects. "No, you're not sorry! You knew exactly what you were doing. Admit it. You were judging my daughter."

I look at her as a dazed deer might look into oncoming headlights. I repeat that I am sorry for the pain I've caused and she repeats, "No, you're not."

I look over at the two other women who came for connection and ended up observing this conflict. I do my best to center us back to the letters, but the damage is already done. The entire atmosphere has been lost as the other two women share their letters. The session ends with the therapist leaving without saying a word.

I have a few moments with the two ladies afterwards and apologize to them both. One of them smiles at me and says, "There was nothing you could do. She was an angry woman."

Her words do not console me because I know I took a risk without considering the consequences. I've done and been part of enough training that I know the ground rules, and I broke them. *Never think that the lesson you have to teach is more important than the other's emotional wellbeing. That's always their decision.*

With fifty-nine sessions ahead of me, I realize I will need to exhibit a lot of compassion for myself. I do not beat myself up. *I royally fucked up my first session, and it's okay.* I am just happy to have learned this now and not later. Although there is power in the exercise, I will need to be more conscious when I bring it forward next time.

As I prepare to leave the bookstore, the manager comes over to me and says, "It's time to settle up." We walk to the register to see the book sales. He types in the name of the book and, lo and behold, two books have been sold. I feel he expects me to be disappointed, but I say, "That's fantastic!"

He looks at me, confused. Little does he know that these are my first book sales and, as strange as it might sound, I didn't even expect that. I sold my first book. It is an incredible feeling. I went from lying under the covers on my honeymoon less than a year earlier—to this. I am incredibly grateful. Sure, my first session was a mess, but there is something beautiful in failing. This trip is not about getting it all right. It is about getting out and doing it.

I've left the comfort of my home and wife to set out on an adventure, and I have two book sales and one failed session behind me. It all feels like a great success.

CHAPTER 3

The Vietnamese Retirement Home

(Seattle, Washington)

*A*fter one of our long walks, Steve mentions that he won't be able to spend time with me the following day because he is volunteering at a retirement community for Vietnamese. I ask, "Why not have a Last Letter session there?"

His eyes light up with a mix of excitement and confusion. He says, "Andy, they don't speak English. How's that going to work?"

I laugh and say, "No problem." If there is one thing that I've learned by traveling for so many years, it is to communicate in the universal language of vulnerability. Managing a session where little English will be spoken isn't something I worry about.

The session is arranged and we arrive at the retirement home. Two of the administrators attend the session to listen and help translate. I count ten people in the room, whose ages appear to range from sixty-five to 100. About half of them don't speak any English.

I can see the people are very welcoming and grateful for our presence. I begin slowly, and I speak in short sentences to make it easy for the translator. I am very connected emotionally and I feel the tears coming up as I share why this exercise is so important to me. "I lost my mom to a drunk driver. She was the most important thing in my life. I wrote a letter to her that she received a few hours before her death. Now I am asking others to take this opportunity to live with that urgency and write to someone they love."

I see tears welling up in the eyes of many of the participants. Others are confused because they were expecting to be cutting paper with scissors in their usual arts and crafts hour. But their confusion quickly turns to participation.

I watch a ninety-seven-year-old woman write with meticulous care. She is wearing plastic gloves and a mask over her face to ward off disease. She writes with such delicacy and determination. After forty-five minutes, she has written three sentences, yet the handwriting is perfect. She continues to focus on her writing.

The first to share is a man who appears to be in his late sixties. He shares that he wrote it to his wife of sixty years, with whom he had never shared how much she meant to him. It's not clear whether she is alive or dead. But I have a feeling she is no longer with him. Tears stream down his face as he shares how important his wife is to him and how grateful he is to have written this letter. Steve and I watch in astonishment as the space opens up with a sense of love and care.

We move to each person one by one, and the story of each builds in both intensity and vulnerability. Sitting across from me is a woman who smiles at me with a love that feels overwhelming.

As I have left myself so vulnerable, I'm far more sensitive to subtle energy. In this case I feel completely seen through. I think to myself, "She really understands that this is an act of love." Her soft eyes don't allow me to pretend otherwise.

She comes in last. She looks at me as if I'm the priest that she will be confessing to. She explains, "I had four children. All of them are no longer alive." I feel my heart sink as I look into her eyes. She wants to feel seen in her suffering and I'm beginning to realize that my role is to sit as witness. To all those that have suffered alone. Quietly.

She continues, "I wrote my letter to my brother who was with me the entire time. He helped me through each death and I'm grateful for his support through the years." The tears roll down her face.

She keeps her eyes glued onto me as if I'm looking into the eyes of my own mother. The love feels overwhelming.

As we close, she gives me a hug that matches the intensity of the gaze of her eyes. In that expression, I feel the depth of acceptance of love, which has always been a challenge for me to accept. Yet on this journey I promise myself that I will give what I receive in equal measure. I hug back with a deep sense of peace. I trust that the universe is giving me what I need at the moment I need it. My only job is to receive it. At this moment, I feel unconditional love from a person I've just met. And it feels incredible.

CHAPTER 4

Forever Not Good Enough

(Portland, OR)

*A*fter spending three days in Seattle, I continue my journey to Portland. I deviate from the straight drive to meander through a set of mountain ranges.

The day before, a massive fire has consumed much of the area. The ground is still smoldering and I can feel the radiant heat as I approach the embers. There have been so many fires in California over the last few years, but I have never seen the devastation firsthand. The strange feeling of death comes over me. I feel the weight of the loss of so much. Then I realize that in a few years, this place will once again be thriving.

I come to visit Nick, whom I met for the first time about six months earlier at a training I gave in northern California. When

I arrive at his house, I meet his wife, Lisa, and their son, Luke. Nick had warned me before I arrived that they were struggling in their marriage. They ask if I might be able to assist.

I am welcomed with great warmth. We sit and we have breakfast together. Nick and Lisa are very reactive to each other. Lisa says, "I am thinking that I am going to start a yoga practice."

Nick is clearly triggered. "Just begin with it," he mutters.

I see a vicious circle of triggers. I can hear the judgment in my head: *He does not trust that she will follow through.* I do what I always do and ask if we can move past the content of the story and discuss the process. I distinguish these two spaces because it is often in the content that people get lost. If I am focused on how to make my point and convince you, it's not very likely that you will feel seen and understood.

I ask both if I can express my observations of triggers. I ask if we can use the triggers to understand the dynamic that is forming. I explain, "I don't care what the story is. I just want to make sure you do not lose one another when you get triggered.

"When you fall into the old pattern, you will find that you move further and further away from one another. My desire would be for you to never get stuck when you are with one another. You don't need to agree, but there is no reason you should lose connection in the process."

I explain that, in my experience, expectations in relationships become a real problem when they go unseen. Especially in the heat of an argument. I point out the triggers over and over again so they can see how they are reacting not to what is being said, but to an expectation they have of one another. Usually this expectation is not even conscious. It's simply a reaction that goes on without reflection.

I came to realize a long time ago that when a relationship is struggling to survive, each side is longing for something. Usually that longing goes unseen and the other is blamed for it when it is missing. Quite ironically, the thing that each one is lacking is rarely being given to the other. So it usually ends up that each person blames the other for exactly the thing they are not giving the other. Each wants to feel seen and understood, but they are not giving that understanding to their partner. Instead, they are often neglecting the other's feelings and consequently pushing them away in the process.

This goes back to the reason why that process is so important. If we stay true to the process, we find we can always assure that our partner feels seen, and therefore remains in connection throughout the interaction. To discuss issues when out of connection tends to compound the problem and does not set an example of how all issues can be solved. It is the difference between simply dealing with the symptom and fundamentally solving the problem.

In this case, Lisa tells me, "I have suffered from depression for many years. I've had a hard time nailing down what I want to be doing with my life."

She has spent years of training in yoga and nutrition. She is clearly intelligent and emotionally aware, but she is lacking self-confidence. She says over and over again, "There are many people far better than myself in the field," and, "I need to complete further training before I can call myself qualified."

This is a phrase that I have become all too accustomed to hear throughout my years as a mentor: "There is one thing I need before I can start." This tends to land in a perpetual cycle of procrastination that leads nowhere. "I need a website." "I need a physical location." "I need a pamphlet." Unfortunately, once that one thing is achieved, there tends to be another thing that becomes the next hurdle.

Nick is seeing the pattern, and yet he is not clear how to deal with it. He wants his wife to succeed. He wants to support her. Yet he sees that continually giving her more and more support is only validating the impediments Lisa is putting in her own way.

The more he tries to point it out, the more tension builds between them. I understand his tension, and at the same time, I understand how it feels to be so insecure to start. You feel like an imposter, teaching something that you, yourself, have just learned.

I ask Lisa if she'll be open to investigating what is behind her beliefs. I see Nick getting very enthusiastic. He is hoping he can leverage my support to move Lisa past her limiting beliefs. I ask Lisa, as I often do, "What's going on?"

She explains that the last two years have not been easy for her. She has had a hard time with her self-confidence. She says, "I have studied these things but I am not good enough to actually charge money for doing them. There are others that are more qualified than I am."

As she speaks, I see Nick in the background vibrating with a palpable intensity. He finally explodes. "There she goes again, saying everything she can't do and not doing anything in the end."

I interrupt my talk with Lisa, who clearly feels unsafe, and turn to Nick. I ask Nick to heighten his attention to what is going on. I explain that this is the exact moment where he loses contact with his wife and alienates her. Although he believes he sees something in his wife's behavior, he is stuck in the content. I ask him to pull back into the process once again.

I ask, "What's going on?"

He replies, "She's always said this, but nothing changes."

I respond, "I understand it's been that way in the past. But behaving this way will most certainly guarantee that it will remain this way in the future. No one wants to be pointed at and told, 'I don't trust you.' It tends to push people away and decrease their limited confidence. In many ways, you are creating this reality by imposing your beliefs on her. You inadvertently have guided the outcome through your behavior."

He understands and settles, which gives me some time to support the dynamic between them. I am coaching two things at once: Lisa's lack of self-confidence and Nick's judgment of it.

As he slows down, the two begin to reflect on the unproductive pattern that's formed between them. I ask him if he will be open to reflect on the moment when he gets triggered. I say, "If nothing else, it will make it impossible to support Lisa."

I also share that I cannot continue if every time I help Lisa overcome an emotional obstruction he chimes in with, "See, I told you." I know my work would be in vain. He agrees and we continue.

I turn back to Lisa and ask, "What are you uncomfortable about?"

She says, "I am not as good as many others that are doing the same thing."

I say, "Clearly, that will always be the case. It's also the case for me. So why is there a problem with that?"

She says, "I want to get it perfect before I start something."

I say, "Yeah, of course we'd all want to get it perfect." But then I ask, "How does getting it perfect stop you from actually getting anything done?"

She admits that for years she's been trying to get it right. To get it perfect. She tells me there is a voice in her head telling her that she isn't good enough. I ask if we can take another step deeper into this.

I ask, "What are some of the things you are worried about if you don't get it perfect?"

She tells me she'd love to give yoga classes but she hasn't done it for quite some time.

I laugh and say, "Wonderful. We're going to start giving yoga classes." I see her whole body recoil at the thought that she might now be forced to do something uncomfortable. I ask, "So why not just do it?"

Again, she says, "I would need to get another certification before I'd be comfortable doing that."

I say, "There's nothing wrong with you getting the certification. But how about offering some classes before, so you can grow and begin to build up some level of confidence?"

Again, she recoils, feeling as if she is going to be put into an uncomfortable position. She isn't happy about that. I don't want to push, so I ask her permission to try something together. I ask, "What is it that you are most frightened to say?"

She says, "I am not a good yoga instructor."

I reply, "How about if we take that a little bit further and say, 'I am a shitty yoga instructor.'"

She looks at me with big, confused eyes. "I can't say that."

I say, "Just give it a try. Allow yourself to say it and feel what it feels like to let that be."

She says again, "I can't say that. I can't say that."

Then we wait in silence. Slowly she builds up her voice and says, "I am a shitty yoga instructor. I am a shitty yoga instructor. I am a shitty yoga instructor."

I then ask her to repeat the same phrase, only this time adding, "And it's okay."

She begins to repeat it, taking a pause between each sentence. "I am a shitty yoga instructor, and it's okay. I am a shitty yoga instructor, and it's okay. I am a shitty yoga instructor, and it's okay."

As she slowly repeats the sentence and feels deeper into the acceptance of it, the fear and anxiety of needing to be perfect is slowly melting. The thought that once dominated her thinking is loosening its grip.

She keeps repeating the phrase. I can see her eyes looking upwards at the corners of the room with an inquisitive gaze. Something is going on, but she can't quite put her finger on it. She laughs and says, "How is it that being okay with being a shitty yoga instructor makes it so much easier?"

She slowly repeats the phrase with wonder. Almost as if she is looking inside her own mind to try and figure out what is going on in there. I say, "Instead of just being okay with it, you could take one more step and say, 'I love it. It's great.'"

"I am a shitty yoga instructor, and it's great. I am a shitty yoga instructor, and I love it." She laughs at the space she has created for herself.

The thought of trying to be a perfect yoga instructor was killing her, and now she is free to just be. Undefined by perfection.

I now ask, "How do you feel about giving courses now?"

As if she is an entirely different person she says, "Well, since I am a shitty yoga instructor, I guess I have nothing more to lose."

"So are you ready to start your courses?" I ask.

She replies, "Yes."

Two days later I receive a text with a thank you. She recognizes she is now free to be whomever she wants and do whatever she wants. She no longer needs to defend or protect around the fear that she isn't good enough.

That solves the challenge regarding her and her professional journey, but it doesn't yet deal with the challenges between the two. The next day, I ask Nick if he wants to reflect on how his behavior has been separating him from Lisa.

He says, "Yes."

I ask, "What happens to you when she talks about these things and you feel as if nothing's going to happen?"

He says, "I get frustrated and then the frustration turns into anger and resentment."

I ask him, "How's that working for you?"

He says, "It's not."

I ask, "Well, what's an alternative?"

He looks puzzled and shrugs his shoulders. "I don't know. What is it?"

I ask, "Before you get angry, what happens inside of you?

Before the frustration comes up. What's the first thing that happens?"

He says, "I feel helpless. I feel incapable. I want to help. But I can't."

I ask him, "What happens when you allow yourself to speak from that space, instead of the anger and frustration?"

I see him sit in wonder. There is a calm that comes over him. "It's vulnerable," he says.

I can see in his eyes that he knows there is a truth but it isn't easy for him to wean himself off the addiction to blame others for his frustration.

He says, "If I spoke from my incapacity it would actually bring us closer together. It would allow me to support Lisa in her journey without excluding myself and my own feelings."

I say, "Wow, that sounds great! Let's try it now. Nick, Lisa's now saying she's going to do something and you're quite sure that she's not. What are you going to do?"

He says, "Lisa, when you speak I feel myself get very uncomfortable. I know that you say that you're going to do this or that, but in the past we've had similar discussions, and I want to support you, but it's hard because I feel like it hasn't gone anywhere. I want to support you but I don't know how."

I can see from Lisa's face that she can see that Nick isn't judging her. He is just sharing his own struggle. She does not respond as she has in the past when she felt Nick was pointing things out in order to force her to see it. He isn't imposing it upon her.

She says, "Yes, I can understand why you'd say that. How would you feel about supporting me there?"

I interrupt. I see that this is a trap that Lisa isn't aware of. I say, "You can't delegate self-discipline. This is something that you'll need to dedicate to yourself. You can't ask someone else to manage that for you. Instead you can tell Nick what you are planning to do and ask him if he could support you in that. When he sees you're not doing it, he can point it out. You keep the agency over your own life, instead of delegating it to Nick and having him take responsibility for your determination."

They both smile because they see how they can quickly create codependency if they make the other responsible for their ambitions. I ask if she can phrase it in a way that takes responsibility and invites support from Nick. She replies, "I commit to taking action in getting these courses arranged. I ask you to support me if you see me not continually taking action in that direction."

Nick is anxious and replies hastily, "In the past when I have brought my concerns to you, you have felt judged and it has become a fight."

I ask him to feel into the insecurity we discussed earlier and try to say the same thing again. He pauses, slows down and says, "Knowing in the past that I have sometimes tried this and it hasn't worked, how can I make sure to do it differently, so I don't trigger you?"

She smiles and says, "Well, do me a favor and bring it forward as you're bringing it forward to me now. I can see you and I don't feel judged."

They both laugh and smile, then hug, happy to have discovered a new approach to communicating with one another.

They ask, "Andy, we don't want to lose this. What rules can we lay down?"

I say, "I can't tell you what to do, but I can certainly tell you what not to do. You will need to break the pattern. Whenever you're triggered, don't fall into the trap. Don't react without consciousness."

Nick says, "I can't guarantee that I am not going to get triggered."

I say, "I certainly hope you do. This isn't about stopping your triggers. It's about how you deal with it the moment you see it happening. The real question is, how willing are you to put your ego aside at the moment you're triggered, and allow yourself to share vulnerability instead of frustration and anger?"

He says, "I am dedicated to doing that."

I then say, "Okay, so if you set up the rules, then what would they be?"

Nick answers, "The first rule would be I no longer accept that I react from a state of being triggered. Then the second rule is when I am triggered, I'll share my incapacity instead of my frustration. And the third rule is that I will listen to everything the other person has to say, without interruption. They must feel completely seen and heard. I won't speak until they feel that they've expressed themselves completely. After they've expressed themselves completely, I will share what I believe I heard and then add whatever it is that I feel might complement what they have said. I won't just be silent and wait for my opportunity to speak, as I have done in the past."

I agree. "If you're not listening to the other person, but rather waiting for them to finish talking so you can make your point, you're not really listening. You're just holding back, but that's not really listening. It's a technique and people can sense it."

I ask them to truly listen to one another. Of course, listening begins by first not reacting unconsciously to triggers. And when we're truly listening, we don't know what our next question will be until we feel it. Our questions do not push people in any direction, but rather help the other get more connected to themselves and thereby clearer on the challenge they are facing. For example: "What's going on with _____? How is that impacting you? How open are you to looking at alternatives at the moment? Would you possibly consider _____? How might I be able to support you in that regard?"

Through such questions, a powerful process of self-discovery occurs. Once we put our egos aside and no longer react from triggers, we begin to see one another. It's here that people see and feel seen. They are no longer trying to win an argument, but rather seek to get closer.

It's very dense.
I hear your advice,
  but don't know how you got it.
From your language I know you
  have a background in healing
  and spirituality —
  but you don't share that,
  so I only have my emotional
  reaction to the transfor-
  mation of the people you
  visit and talk too
You present yourself as a
healer, not as a teacher.
And the radical self love
  journey is not in here yet.
  (which is the link I am
    missing)

CHAPTER 5

"I Hate You for Making Me Feel This Way!"

(Bend, Oregon)

The drive from Portland to Bend, Oregon takes two hours. I don't know anyone here, but the Spiritual Community of the Cascades in Bend was one of the first places to respond to my cold emails. I'll always be grateful for that because it was that "yes" that gave me a sense that this strange plan of mine just might work.

When I arrive, I learn that many changes have occurred since our email exchange. Including the fact that the person who agreed to the session has quit. Or got fired. It is all full of mystery. I later come to find out that there was a high turnover in leadership. Apparently, the spiritual community is struggling to figure out whose spirituality they will be adopting. As I am told when I arrive, "Each of the leaders has put forward their own approach, which has been met with resistance from others in the group."

I know this struggle from my past. Put several people who practice "spirituality" in a room together and you are sure to get into an argument.

A week prior to the session, I received a call from the acting director who asked me, "What exactly are you planning to do?" I had the impression that with all the tension in the group, it could be problematic if I would be offering yet another viewpoint on spirituality. They've had enough of those already.

I responded that I'd be sharing my life story and inviting people to write a letter to a loved one. I immediately felt a calm come over her. She explained to me that with all the shifts in leadership there had been fewer gatherings, so mine was going to be the first in a while. She couldn't guarantee any attendees. There was still some animosity from the shakeup.

I arrive about an hour early. The city of Bend is quaint and welcoming. The kind of place where a person would move to get away from the hustle and bustle of the city. This is not the only spiritual community in the area. There are a few.

The community building is old, but well kept. It reminds me of a church in the '70s. There is a lot of wood paneling on the interior walls to complement the surroundings. The director arrives. She has a severe migraine, so I do my best to set up quietly.

As always, I set up in a large circle. She estimates more than twenty people will show. She is spot on. It is the largest group so far and there is a moment of unease as I think how speaking to more people might change how I share my experience.

In the end, it doesn't. I am learning that no matter how large the group, I can still stay with my emotions. The tears arise as I speak and I speak through them with a love and care that shows I am taking care of myself as well as the group.

The group is warm and caring. I see that they truly understand what I am doing, and I see gratitude reflected back in their eyes. All with the exception of one woman, who sits to my right. I am not quite sure what to make of her as she stares at me with a mix of skepticism and curiosity. As I have already decided early on, I will accept everything that appears, and apparently, there is someone who I am triggering in some way. At least, that is what I think.

We break into the letter-writing portion of the exercise and people write for the next forty-five minutes. As we come back together in a circle, I am curious how the dynamic will function, given the size of the group. Will anyone be willing to show vulnerability in a group this size? Especially with the tension here.

I say, "It's not required that anyone read what they wrote, but it would be nice if you shared who you wrote to and why."

One man blurts out, "I'd like to read my letter." There is an urgency in his voice and it is clear that he needs to get it off his chest.

I look at him and say, "Please do."

He begins, "I have written to my wife. I will be meeting her after this event and I have written a letter to her to tell her I want a divorce."

You can cut the air with a knife. Eyes wander between participants checking to see if we've all heard him correctly. I look on, emotionless, as to give him all the space that he needs. He clearly doesn't have any problem taking it.

He reads,

Dear Maggy,
I love you. I have always loved you. I have just come to realize that love is not enough.

We met as two individuals and we developed into two very different ones. I can't tell you how hard it is for me to acknowledge it, but we are not meant to be together. Our lives are following different paths and I have done my best to manage it, but I can't do it any longer.

He continues to read his letter as the group sits as a silent witness. It feels as if we are all taking part in a sacred moment. A moment where he comes to grips with the helplessness of his reality. A moment to make a resolution in front of twenty people who can hold space for him. (I often use the term "holding space," meaning allowing people to share strong or vulnerable feelings without reacting or moving away because we feel uncomfortable. It's companioning people in their suffering, without trying to fix them or change their feelings. Just sitting with their feelings in compassion.)

With tears in his eyes, he finishes reading his letter to the group. There is a long silence. I have resolved not to interrupt silence on this trip. There is something soothing being in a shared space with no words to dilute the intensity of the moment.

That does not stop one man from doing what I see many men like to do: make suggestions. He says, "Are you sure about this? What are the alternatives that you might consider?"

Before it goes too far, I notice that my surrender does have its limits. I say, "If possible, I'd ask that we use this as a moment to listen and allow. In this session, we are witnesses. We are not here to heal anyone."

The man looks back at me in appreciation and I let the group settle before we continue. In order to break the ice going forward, I smile and say, "Who would like to go next?"

They laugh as if the air is being let out of a balloon. Then from the corner of the room, the director says, "Everyone, take a deep breath." She does this a few times during the session. I see that it is a powerful way to settle the energy that has built up during the session.

One by one, we go through the group until we come upon the skeptical-looking woman. Because she does not reveal much, I am not sure if she will even want to share who she has written to. I am happy to move past her if she is not comfortable. This is not the case.

She looks at me square in the eyes and says, "I hate you! I hate you for making me feel this way."

I look at her with love and gratitude. She has finally revealed herself. I sit quietly until she composes herself to continue. She says, "I don't want to feel these feelings. My husband committed suicide in front of me and my daughter was murdered. I have had enough death in my life." And then she let the tears come.

I am unaware of it at the time, but she plays a powerful role in the group. She is the author of many books, and she is one of the individuals that has created tension in the community. In this moment, the group finally has the opportunity to see her. Not the author and coach façade, but the inner child who has been hiding beneath.

I can sense the dynamic shift immediately. There is a loosening that occurs within the group. It is like a reset button has been pressed and they have a chance to see one another in their humanity. Not to discuss spirituality as a concept, but to live it as a group.

We close the session and many participants hug me with deep appreciation, including the director. She says, "You can never imagine the gift you have given our community. You were a light in the darkness."

I walk her to her car. In the parking lot I find the man in

the group who was quick to offer suggestions. He introduces himself as Jim, but he is quick to tell me his Tibetan lama name is Ngawang (*NGAH-wahng*), which means "powerful speech." This should not have been a surprise. He has an unsettled energy around him, as if he is dying to have an audience. But he is quick to see his own limitations. "I could never do what you just did. Nothing of you needed to show up. I still need some degree of recognition. I am not ready to completely let go."

As he speaks, and he speaks a lot, he tells me that as a child he was visited by Buddhist lamas. They came from the Himalayas to tell him that he was the ancestor of a great lama and he was sent to Bend to support the spiritual community here. This gives me some indication of his need to speak during the session earlier. He wasn't just talking. He was fulfilling his destiny.

As he speaks, I cannot tell if anything he is saying has actually occurred. I am so entertained that I am just enjoying the surreal image I have in my head of lamas showing up at his door as a child and telling him he was a long-lost ancestor.

He rattles off name after name of guru and healer. I have heard of most, even if I'm not able to say much about them. I tell him that my mentor was a big fan of Krishnamurti and he gasps. "I could have guessed that from how you lead the group."

I am not exactly sure what he means, nor do I ask.

He asks, "How would you feel if I joined you along the route? I'll just leave everything as is and head off with you. It will be like groupies on a Grateful Dead tour. We can gather people one session at a time and we'll end up with a few hundred by the end."

I feel my insides jump at the thought that I would be coming with an entourage. I say, "Thank you for the incredible trust, but there is something solemn about this journey. I am not quite sure what I have been sent to learn, but I am guessing that it's not going to be like a rock concert."

We both laugh and he doesn't press the point. In the end, I thank him for an incredibly entertaining evening and head to my hotel. As I drive, I think to myself that if this is any indication of the type of people that I will be meeting, this trip is going to feel more like a carnival side show.

CHAPTER 6

I Left My Head in San Francisco

(San Francisco, California)

I make my way from Oregon to San Francisco, where a friend of mine is hosting a session. My friend introduces me to a young man named Alton. Alton is unlike anyone I've ever met. He explains to me that he has a hard time recognizing emotions. Although he doesn't use the term, it seems to me that perhaps he has some degree of Asperger's syndrome.

He says, "My entire life I have not been able to understand emotions in others. I have spent a lot of time deconstructing the emotional states of others so I could better understand how they work."

To achieve this, Alton goes to extremes. He sits at the dinner table with a GoPro camera hanging around his neck. He explains to me he wears it every time he leaves the house and records all his interactions so he can go back and review them later. He hangs a wooden sign below that camera that says, "Say hello to my little lifelogging project." This is to give fair warning to those who may not be comfortable being filmed.

He is very eager to learn and asks a lot of questions. I see in Alton something I will later come to recognize throughout my time in San Francisco: an incessant need to continually learn. On the surface, it appears to be admirable. But underneath it I see a trap: to not learn is to fail.

In Alton's case, I recognize he is overcoming a personal struggle. He explains to me that his motivation is to share what he learns with his network of close friends. He is so fixated on trying to learn that he doesn't see that sometimes the solution might be to stop searching for a solution. Or simply put, loving something as it is without needing to understand the concept behind it.

When Alton asks me what I do, I reply, "I help people live in the moment."

"How do you do that?" he asks.

"By not responding to questions like that," I answer.

He looks puzzled and checks his camera to make sure it is recording.

I smile and say, "See how you're confused right now?"

"Yes."

"Well, that's exactly the space we now share. The difference between the two of us is that I am at peace with that confusion. Where you see confusion, I see clarity."

His face registers the paradox of what I have just said. "That doesn't make any sense."

I reply, "No, it doesn't. But apparently, it does."

He only becomes more confused. I ask, "What if confusion is the solution? What if you saw that confusion is the foundation of everything, and trying to solve it was actually the problem?"

"But how can confusion be a solution?" he asks.

I laugh and say, "What if you observed the confusion and did not try to make any sense of it? Just let it be as it is. We are all confused. And that's not comfortable, so we try to control it. We try to take command over our thoughts. We define and create logical structures, models, principles, equations, and diagrams to make sense of our thoughts and emotions.

"But just because we've made a mental model doesn't mean we are more able or capable of living or feeling that raw emotional experience. It just means we have the perception that we understand the thought or experience better. It gives our mind some rest, because living with all the confusion is exhausting.

"Or is it? Instead of trying to understand everything, see how it feels if you just allow your brain to observe the activity, without trying to do anything with it."

Alton says, "That's meditation."

I reply, "Then make your life a meditation. Observe your thoughts without being them. See how things change when you are no longer driven by your incessant thoughts. This is just confusion. And since I'm okay with confusion, I don't try to control my brain anymore. I just study it as it produces a lot of noise. Apparently, that's what it does. Try for a moment to just observe the world without trying to create or impose a mental, logical structure on it."

I can see Alton understands me, at least logically. But he is struggling with the implications of living that way. He says, "If I was to accept what you're now telling me, I don't know how I could exist in the world. The only way I do exist is by understanding how the mental constructs work. I create structures that make them more and more transparent."

"I would never want to take that ability away from you," I clarify. "I just want you to complement it with another ability, which is to see through your need to do that."

We are often driven to certain thoughts and behaviors out of a desire to control. Control is not bad. But if that desire goes unanalyzed and unchecked, it actually means that we are controlled by our need to control. The need to understand and explain emotions can become its own confusion.

There is a freedom in the ability to consciously change our emotional states in order to improve our well-being. And I've found an even deeper freedom: the freedom to observe emotional experiences just as they are, with no desire to change or control them.

CHAPTER 7

Reflecting on a Life of Privilege

(San Francisco, California)

Late in the evening, I get a message from an old college friend. She invites me to meet for breakfast in the middle of San Francisco.

I wake the next morning and head to the Panera Bread on King Street, where I meet up with my friend. We spend a half hour laughing about the past and catching up on the present. She leaves and I pull out my computer to read some emails.

Soon afterward, a black couple comes and sits at the table next to me. The tables are so close to one another that we'll be able to hear each other. I smile and nod at them as they sit.

I read and respond to emails for the next half hour, until I hear something that catches my attention. The man tells the woman, "You need to wipe the top of your drink before you sip it. Canned drinks are the dirtiest thing you come into contact with in a restaurant."

She says, "How? They're sealed."

He replies, "Yes, but mice crawl over the tops of all of the cans and they pee. It's dirty and dangerous."

Because I once managed a restaurant, I have some experience with mice and soft drinks. I chime in, "Yes, he's right. It's quite possibly the dirtiest thing in a restaurant."

I can tell they feel comfortable with me and we strike up a conversation, which ranges from being black in America to living your passion. The woman's name is Leslie. She is thirty-two years old, from Georgia, and a mother of two. At some point in our conversation, she looks at me and with a soft openness asks, "Would you mind if I share my story with you?"

I smile and say, "I'd love to hear it."

Leslie shares that she is adopted, but she doesn't want to be pitied. "This is where I came from, but it will not define me," she says.

What strikes me about Leslie is that she is actively shaping her life. I can see from the way she speaks that she is trained. Everything is measured. Her questions are part of a script. Her manner of speaking and behavior don't seem to come naturally to her. Yet one thing is clear: From her training, she has learned how to create rapport. I can see she is very genuine in her effort to make a difference in her own and her children's lives. I am in awe. I can see that by nature she is loud, chaotic, and fun-loving. She has clearly learned how to engage in a way that makes one feel appreciated, seen, and understood.

What catches me most is the way she summarizes everything I say to show she has fully listened. She asks me, "What is the one thing you would recommend I do to succeed?"

I laugh and say, "Continue doing what you are doing."

Through these questions she is demonstrating her dedication, her discipline. She then asks, "What guides you to make a difference in the world?"

"Love," I say.

She looks surprised and says it is the first time she's heard that. The answer is usually money, children, or family. She explains, "I want to be a radiologist technician. I need to earn enough points selling magazines so I can do that."

Leslie tells me she wakes up every morning at seven a.m. to go door-to-door asking people if they will be interested in buying magazines. She travels around the country and works thirteen-hour days. She is not allowed to accept donations. She can only sell magazines because, as she puts it, "I am here to create value. Not to take handouts based on pity from others."

I am now on a book tour around the US hoping to change peoples' lives. Leslie is on her own tour to change the lives of her two sons. She has taken disadvantage in life and turned it into something that could compel her to grow, learn, and reach her fullest potential.

I say, "I can't imagine you not being successful."

While conversing, something hits me. I've always known it, but now it is right in front of me. I see all the privilege I have been afforded my entire life. It's hard to see because it's like the water in which fish swim. But I see it clearly as Leslie speaks.

I see the jobs I got without having the proper qualifications. The benefit of the doubt I was given in difficult situations. The trust that was placed upon my opinion. All these things are subtle yet very real. I've benefited from them my entire life. And now I'm sitting in front of someone who has not been afforded the same privileges. In fact, many of the things I've taken for granted my whole life are daunting challenges for her.

I'm traveling through the US just days before the midterm elections. In political discourse, I often hear things like, "Nothing was handed to me. I earned all this. I didn't get to where I am by sitting and waiting to get paid."

Of course, in many cases there's truth to that statement. But I also see that in a life of unseen, unspoken privilege, nothing is given *per se*. It is implicit in the system. We don't see how things are different for others because we make the flawed assumption that our lives are just like everyone else's. Describing privilege is like describing air to a fish. If you live in water, air is a foreign concept.

I'm inspired by Leslie's determination and dedication. She is dedicated to making her life successful, putting in the time, effort and energy to overcome what appears to be a difficult childhood. I realize how easy my childhood was in contrast. How easy it was for me to go to college and have it paid for. How easy it was for me to decide to travel around the world and have people pay me for odd jobs. I have always been in a position of advantage just because of my skin color. Because of my financial background. Because of my accent that is considered normal. Because of the clothes my parents could afford to buy for me. Because of the health care that allowed me to have straight, white teeth.

Before leaving, I give Leslie a book and a hug and thank her for being an inspiration. I feel a deep humility as I see that we are given gifts in life and we have a chance to embrace them at any moment. I am now surrendering to my own. The opportunities that my advantage has afforded me are now being shared.

CHAPTER 8

Crying on TV

(San Francisco, California)

A week before I arrived in San Francisco, a friend, who had done a book tour years ago, asked me, "How many morning TV shows have you arranged?"

Before he asked me this question, I had no intention of trying to make it on TV. But after his question I thought, *I would be stupid not to try.* I asked if he would send me a copy of the proposal he used. I adapted it and sent it out to a few TV stations in San Francisco. I was not sure what would come of it. I was shocked to receive a reply within two hours. The largest morning show in the Bay Area wanted me as a guest.

Now I'm in San Francisco and the day of the interview arrives. I am both scared and excited. It will be the first time I am on TV and I am not really sure what to expect. I give myself an extra hour in the morning to prepare. I don't want to leave anything to chance.

As I look through my clothes, I can't find any pants. It dawns on me that I left my stack of pants at the last place I stayed. All my pants are now a nine-hour drive away. I now have just over an hour to get to the TV studio. I feel the panic set in and then I begin to laugh. *Well, I have never let the absurd stop me before, so why now?* I think.

I make peace with the fact that I'll be strolling into the studio in shorts, and begin to gather my things. As I am heading out the door, I realize there's a closet I didn't check in my friend's house. I check it and, sure enough, I find a pair of beige polyester slacks from the eighties.

I get in my car and drive across the Bay Bridge to the studio in Oakland. Before arriving, I find a spot nearby for a coffee and a muffin. I take a deep breath and remind myself that this trip is all about surrender, and this is just one more thing to surrender to. I arrive at the studio with fifteen minutes to spare. I see the security guard who pointed me to the coffee shop fifteen minutes earlier. As I come through the gates, he mentions that he left his muffin on the coffee shop counter earlier that day.

Something in me feels compelled to drive back to get it for him. I am supposed to be on TV in a few minutes, and yet this man who was so kind to me moments earlier could use some help. It feels like a test. If I leave at this moment, I risk missing my opportunity to be on TV. But if I miss the opportunity to help this man, I miss the opportunity to be present in this moment.

Without another thought, I turn the car around and head back to the coffee shop. It takes a bit longer than I anticipated because I have to stop for a long train. When I arrive at the coffee shop, a line has formed. I take a few deep breaths and laugh inside. If I miss this opportunity because I pick up this muffin, it will be beautiful. It will be exactly how I want to live this trip. Not fighting for an outcome but staying with what is important in the moment.

I explain my predicament to people in line. They all are very supportive as I get the muffin and head back to the TV station. I hand the muffin off to a very appreciative guard, and it feels like I've set the atmosphere for the rest of my day.

In the studio I'm greeted by a woman, and I can tell somehow that she has worked here for years. I ask, "How long have you worked here?"

"Over twenty-five years," she replies. I have a strange ease come over me. I look at the entire thing from her perspective, which immediately puts me back into my skin. I am looking at this as if it is something special. She sees this as another day at the office.

I sign all the waivers and I am guided to a sofa in a corner of the studio. There is nothing separating me from the interviewers. Twenty seconds before we go live, I am ushered into my chair. The next thing I know, we're on the air. My interviewers are two men in suits, which feels off. We'll be talking about emotions but it looks like a job interview.

It is clear that one is more comfortable with the content than the other. The one man has had loss in this own life and says he chose the story because it touched him. The other seems to be more comfortable with a lighter story. I can tell because he smiles a lot when emotional subjects come up.

The interview goes on for about five minutes, and then the more interested interviewer hits me with a question that takes the breath out of me: "If you had known your mother was going to die, what would you have written differently to her?"

I turn quiet and my eyes water. Again, I promise myself that I am not going to step away from my emotions. Just because I now have a TV camera pointing at me, that is not going to change things.

I let the tears form and am not concerned with the quiet. I can see the man isn't quite sure if I can continue. Before he moves on to another question I say, "I would have told her, I am going to miss you."

Those are the hardest words for me to say. They have always been. "I miss you" is an admission that something cannot be solved. Something that is emotionally vulnerable. I go on to share how hard it is to imagine the loss of someone you love and that it's virtually impossible to imagine the pain.

I can see that the two men are now also on the verge of tears as we look at one another. As I leave, they both get up and give me a hug. I feel as if we've had a special moment in the middle of their normal, routine day. Later that day I receive an email from the program director who shares that she reviewed several emails sent in gratitude that they aired the story. She forwards me one that says, "I am feeling very lonely and I really needed this story today. Thank you for airing it."

CHAPTER 9

Visiting Dad

(Monterey, California)

*M*y next stop is Monterey, California. Monterey is an important stop for me because it's where my father retired and died.

I visited him once while he lived there and once for the funeral. I am very much looking forward to visiting my dad's chosen home for the last years of his life, and writing him a letter during the next session. I feel a connection to this area. This will be a celebration of my dad and what he meant to me. I am also feeling appreciation for him.

Oftentimes, when I've shared my relationship with my dad with others, it was from the perspective of the younger Andy who was very resentful of him. When he died, I was over that. I had learned to love him with all of his incapacities—sometimes even because of those incapacities. In a strange way, I feel like I've been throwing my dad under the bus. Because if I were to share how I really felt about him just before he died, it would be a very different story.

I find a wonderful bookstore, The Old Capital, that is willing to host a session. It feels like I am stepping back in time. There are eight rows of massive bookshelves. Each shelf runs the length of the store, which is quite long.

On the day of the session I walk in and see the store is empty. With all of the space the books take up, it feels even emptier. But it's fine because my session isn't for another half hour.

I introduce myself to the man behind the counter. He isn't prepared, which gives me an indication of what is to come. I ask, "How many people usually show up for these things?"

He says, "It varies."

It feels like a polite way of saying, "Possibly no one."

I prepare, like I do for all the sessions, by setting up my camera on a tripod. I sit and wait. Five minutes turn into ten, ten turn into twenty. No one shows up. All the while I record myself alone at the table.

Instead of feeling shame or a need to prove or present myself in another light, I get the greatest joy from sharing the wonder of this moment on social media. Me sitting alone at a table with no one to join me. I caption it: "Highlights from last night's session." The video receives more likes than any other that I have posted. After making it onto the most viewed morning show in the Bay Area a day earlier, I am now sitting alone in Monterey.

I keep thinking, *What a success this has all been.* On social media we only see people in their positive light. Of course, this can give others the impression that they are more successful, talented, or wealthy than they really are. I believe that our inability to celebrate all parts of life is exactly the thing that stops us from truly cherishing it. Trying to present ourselves in a particular light doesn't allow us to fully embrace who we are at every moment.

My desire on this trip is to be an example of the thing I am asking others to be. Not to be cool. Not to be successful. But to be vulnerable. To be worthy of the hashtag I chose— #inspirevulnerability. When things go well, to scream from the mountaintops, "Success is not the outcome of any endeavor, but being in the world and cherishing every moment, regardless of what the outcome is!" And when I am sitting alone behind a table in a local bookstore, to share that, too. When we fail to celebrate these two equally, we make ourselves dependent on the goal, failing to realize it was all about the journey.

After waiting for another half hour, I give up. I leave the bookstore and walk across the street to a coffee shop. I get my coffee and sit in the corner. I see a frail, elderly gentleman drinking coffee and reading the newspaper. I can see he spends a lot of time in the coffee shop looking for company.

He introduces himself as James and asks me what I'm doing there. I tell him I've just come from the bookstore where no one showed up for my event. He smiles and says, "Apparently, you were meant to be here with me." He asks me what I'm doing with my trip, which I explain. "That's beautiful," he says.

He then goes on to tell me that ten years ago, his son wrote him a letter. "It was the most important thing I have ever received," he says. He tells me that he never felt like he had been a good father. He wasn't as present as he would have liked. He owned a business and he spent most of his time at the office making money.

He says, "I feel like I confused taking care of the family with making money."

I share with him that I had a similar experience with my father. "It sounds like I was your child," I say, laughing.

James continues, "I had some strange idea that there would never be enough money to take care of all of their needs. I always needed to earn more. In his letter, my son told me that everything he had learned and accomplished in life was the result of the lessons he learned from me. When I read that, I broke into tears. I wasn't perfect but I gave him everything he needed to succeed in life."

He's crying now. And then he says, "My son died in a car accident two years ago. It has not been easy. No one should have to bury their own child."

We sit and share a deep appreciation for one another. He thanks me for what I am doing and for the people I am supporting. He also thanks me for reminding him about his son during this strange chance meeting. We hug each other as if we have known one another for years, and I continue on to my hotel.

It dawns on me that James is about the same age as my father would have been if he were still alive. There is something beautiful about letting go of what I thought this day was supposed to be and instead, embracing a beautiful moment with a man who took the place of my dad for an hour. We both miss someone special in our lives. He, his son, and me, my father.

CHAPTER 10

Heartbeats in Esalen

(Big Sur, California)

A week before I arrived in San Francisco, a friend asked me if
I wanted to spend a few days with him in Esalen and hold
a few sessions there. I knew nothing about the location, except
that it was in Big Sur. I did a quick Google search and discovered
that it's the epicenter of alternative and spiritual practices that
began in the sixties.

After I finish in San Francisco, I head to Esalen. When I
arrive, I don't know exactly what is expected of me. My friend
started a global organization with the purpose of transforming
human consciousness. He was awarded a grant to have people
get acquainted with biofeedback technology. To get data for
biofeedback study, several sensors are attached to participants'

bodies, with the purpose of exploring how technology can amplify the experience of connection to oneself and between individuals in groups. The idea is simple. If you can measure a heartbeat and EKG responses, then you can translate that into a meaningful experience for participants.

The challenge is not the technology, which has existed for many years. Rather, it's how to translate it into a meaningful experience. This is where I am supposed to come in. I see a mass of wires on the floor and I am told I will be giving my session in an hour and a half. I have not tested the technology, yet I'll soon be leading a session.

I get curious, close my eyes and think, *What would intrigue me? How can I create an experience where people might sense a loss of their own identity?* This is often referred to as transpersonal, where people experience themselves beyond their own self-identity.

I decide to play it safe and use my first session to play with the technology. I think it will be nice to create ceremony around individuals' relationships to their hearts. It's an opportunity to show gratitude for something that most of us take for granted. They have headphones on so they can hear their own heartbeat. In addition, there are lights that beat to the rhythm of their heart.

The experience is more powerful than I would have expected. It's beautiful to watch as people become acquainted with their hearts. One participant says, "It has been working all these years and I have never been grateful for it." Another says, "As I hear it, I realize that one day it will stop beating."

I think it will be nice to amplify the experience by allowing participants to share their heartbeats with one another. Once again, the experience turns out to be more powerful than I could have imagined. Tears are streaming down many of the participants' faces as they hand over their blinking hearts and hear the heartbeat of their partner in their headphones.

The humor is that although most have never heard their own heart before, they sit in judgment of it. "It's too fast," one woman says. Others sit and marvel that there is something inside of themselves they aren't acquainted with, something that has played such a vital role in their existence.

Once the people receive their hearts back and we finish the exercise, everybody shares how hard it was to share their hearts with others. How much challenge there was in allowing one to be fully seen in their vulnerability. There is a deepening of contact that most people have never experienced before.

As a final exercise, I ask for participants to share their experience with the group. We all have our hearts reflected by the blinking lights in front of us. I ask each participant to use the symbolism of this moment to raise their beating heart lights above their head. His or her heart can be played over the loudspeaker and everyone will hear that single person's heart. I invite them: "While sharing your heartbeat with the group, take a moment to get something off your chest. Something that has been weighing heavy on your heart. Something you have been holding back emotionally."

One by one, each participant lifts the light high. Each heart is shared with the group and each shares what he or she wants to let go of. One person shares, "I want to let go of my self-judgment." Another shares, "I want to let go of feeling the need for perfection." And another shares, "I want to let go of the animosity I have towards my father." It is an incredible moment that, although totally disconnected from my last letter-writing exercise, is just as powerful.

The letters are just a different way of getting something off one's chest. Something that is weighing on people's hearts. I have the opportunity to give people an experience to let go of something in a symbolic gesture using technology. Where technology often separates us from our emotions, here it brings us closer.

CHAPTER 11

A Pending Divorce

(Big Sur, California)

While at Esalen, I spend a lot of time with my friend who arranged the event. He has just recently decided to divorce his wife. She is still hoping things might get patched up. He wants to redefine his life, but he isn't exactly sure how to go about doing that. He knows he isn't happy, and he can't quite articulate exactly what isn't working for him.

In spite of this, he knows something needs to change. The breakup isn't messy, but by the same token, like any breakup, it is uncomfortable. He can't share with his wife the exact reason for the separation. He just knows it needs to happen. This leads to a lot of confusion.

I have seen that people who have a strong resolve, but an

inability to share what's going on inside of them, create confusion. Most people want, or even need, to understand the reasons for a separation. Simply saying, "It does not work for me," does not calm the insatiable need to understand to know, "What did I do wrong?" or "What could I have done differently?"

I help him come to peace with his own resolve. What that means is accepting his situation without judgment for himself or his soon-to-be ex-wife. When people do not feel at peace with a decision, they tend to procrastinate. In these moments, it's almost impossible to reflect meaningfully on ourselves.

When we ask ourselves, "What did I do wrong?" it is almost impossible to see what has created the situation to begin with. Guilt sets in and there is little or no space for self-reflection. The deepest self-reflection always comes when the voices of judgment are settled.

In order to help my friend calm his internal voices, I ask him to feel into the emotions he is resisting. "What is the hardest thing for you to say?" I ask. He is confused. "Just say the thing that is hardest to admit," I repeat.

"I gave up my life. I followed the desires of someone else. Not my own."

I think to myself what that translates into. I offer, "How about saying, 'I have never taken responsibility for my own life.'"

He repeats the sentence, "I have never taken responsibility for my own life."

I ask him to repeat the same sentence but this time add, "And it's okay."

"I can't say that," he says.

I reply, "Just say it and feel what it does for you. You are allowing yourself to play with your subconscious. As you speak the words out, you'll either feel if they are true to you, or you will feel the true feelings. The feelings that become apparent when you feel the contrast in yourself."

He begins repeating the sentence over and over again, adapting it to feel into the different areas where he has been feeling constriction. "I was manipulated into this marriage and it's okay." "I have been living someone else's life and it's okay." And on and on. I can see he is loosening up.

He mentions that he met another woman while at Esalen. Although nothing inappropriate happened, he is feeling guilty because he has feelings for her. I ask him to feel into the shame and guilt and, using the same technique, allow himself to release— naming the resistance and reclaiming it by embracing it.

I leave him feeling more grounded in his emotion. But I know that this will be a difficult journey for his soon-to-be ex-wife. I know his confusion will not be easy for her to process. I feel a sense of helplessness that I won't be able to also support her. I've learned from my own experience that our confusion is not only painful for us, but for those we leave in our wake.

CHAPTER 12

The Angry Professor Melts

(Big Sur, California)

I wake up the next morning and prepare for my next Esalen session. This session is a bit different. A woman walks in, angry and irritated. As she sits down to my right, her eyes roam. It's apparent she feels no sense of peace or belonging here. It takes twenty minutes to attach all the electronic equipment we're using for the session, and I can feel her agitation building.

It goes from bad to worse when she asks if she can sit in a chair instead of on the floor. The organizer replies, "You can't do that."

She says, "I am not comfortable on the floor."

He grudgingly sets up a chair. Her face communicates her frustration. It's now my responsibility to give her the sensation of being one with everything. Good luck to me!

I go through the session as I have before. About twenty-five minutes in, she gets up and leaves. It is abrupt, and lacks any consciousness that her departure might disturb the group. I see that her challenges are bigger than any reaction she might be giving me. I do not take it personally. Surrendering means that I even get to appreciate and accept the challenges other people are wrestling with. I give her a smile of acknowledgement as she gets up and leaves.

The next day, I see her out walking. I wave to her to ask if we can speak. There is something about her that tells me she is strong and doesn't want to be bullshitted. Before I can put the words back in my mouth, I blurt, "Why were you being such a bitch yesterday?" I say it with love and care, which completely disarms her. It's as if I am showing love for the thing that others and she herself judged.

Her eyes widen, then she breaks into a smile. I can see her asking herself, *Is this guy for real?*

She sits down next to me and we spend the next couple of hours talking. She is surprised that I'm so comfortable engaging her with such openness. I tell her, "You can do your best to push people away with your hard exterior. But I see through that."

She tells me she was a professor at University of California San Francisco. She also shares that all her life she has been judged for her abruptness. I laugh and say, "Of course you have."

She looks puzzled. "What do you see?"

I answer, "When you leave a group and don't explain yourself, you leave it to everyone else to interpret how you are feeling. I guarantee you, they're not interpreting in your favor."

She asks, "What's the alternative?"

"Well, given that your facial expressions speak volumes, sharing a little bit about what's going on for you before you leave will help people see you."

We go on to discuss where this is showing up in all aspects

of her life. She works through how she can move through each situation differently going forward.

She inquires, "Why are people so judgmental?"

"It's in our nature," I say. "Don't ask why. Just consider what you can do so that it's no longer your issue, or at least makes it less of an issue for you."

An opportunity for her to practice this arises quickly. We meet the following day and she tells me about a session she attended earlier that day. Not surprisingly, she was at odds with the trainer.

I ask, "How did you deal with it?"

She says, "Well, usually I would have gotten up and left, like I did at your session. This time I shared what was not working for me and we interacted around it. I ended up staying and enjoying it."

She is deeply appreciative, as if I have given her a key to a door that she has waited to open for some time. I give her a copy of *The Last Letter* and she asks me question after question.

When I look back at how we became close so quickly, I see that it was because I followed my intuition. I could have showed myself to her in so many different ways. It's obvious to see that people could easily judge my use of the word "bitch." But it was exactly because I used that word, and not something more diplomatic, that she trusted me. It was a way of breaking through social norms. Obviously, when we do this, there's no guarantee it will be interpreted the way it was intended. And it certainly won't work with everyone. But in this moment, it was the most appropriate thing to do.

All her life, she has felt judged by the world. But no one ever interacted with her around those judgments. I show her that she can be loved for exactly the thing she is being judged for. She and I exchange phone numbers, and speak throughout my trip. It is a beautiful friendship that began when she got up and left my session without a word.

CHAPTER 13

"Fuck You and Your Judgment."

(Big Sur, California)

At Esalen, I meet a neuroscientist who is working on the same biofeedback project as my friend. She is there to develop a system to measure the state of emotional connection in participants. From the moment we meet, I am very open with her. I feel as if I have met an old friend and I treat her as such. I don't see that this openness is more than she is able to receive.

In the past I would have held myself back in order to meet people where they are. I didn't want to risk making them feel uncomfortable. I would have accommodated their incapacity by speaking a little bit less lovingly or being a little bit less open. But I am beyond that right now.

One evening, we all head to nearby hot springs. Clothing is

optional, and she wears her swimsuit. Since it's a pitch-black night, I laugh at the irony that it's impossible to see her, even with her swimsuit on. My observation clearly does not land with her, and I can tell I've hit a trigger. She's uncomfortable and becomes defensive. My words were not ill-intended, but it doesn't matter.

I know these wounds run deep and I do not want to press her buttons. But her pain is palpable and undeniable. Ever since my mother was killed, I have been acutely sensitive to other people's emotions. And since I have spent most of my life trying to manage my emotions, I see that process clearly in others as well. The neuroscientist presented herself as open, but she left no space for true vulnerability.

I am fully aware at this point that our relationship will go one of two ways: Either she will reflect on what I said that made her feel uncomfortable and allow it to bring us closer together, or she will judge me and react defensively. In my experience, in moments of discomfort, most people turn to judgment. Words like "appropriate" and "inappropriate" are dropped with ease as people move away from their own discomfort and project it onto others.

In my current state of vulnerability and openness, I don't feel like holding space for someone who wants to use me as a punching bag to get rid of her own discomfort. I have self-sacrificed to make others feel more comfortable enough to know it's unfulfilling. I choose not to make it my problem and thus accommodate her insecurity. I've learned from other situations like this that it's pretty hopeless to defuse the tension. So I move on. In the past, I would have spent more time, and let her incapacity absorb my energy and attention. At this moment, I'm happy to be sitting in one of the most beautiful locations I've ever been, gazing up at the stars.

The next day she is incredibly cold to me. I have grown accustomed to this throughout the years. My work is to engage people in very emotionally uncomfortable spaces. So there's a lot of tension when people resist. I don't have a problem with her aloofness. But I also don't pretend like there's nothing going on. I smile at her with love. No need to do anything. Just be there.

The next day, I'm sitting on a bench overlooking the Pacific Ocean, and she comes and sits next to me. She asks, "Are you open to feedback?"

For the first time in my life, I say, "No." I can tell that whatever advice she has for me isn't coming from a genuine place, so I'm not interested.

She is surprised, but I continue, "I am not interested in feedback from someone who is judging me. You can tell me how I made you feel so that we can better understand one another. But I am not interested in you telling me what you think."

Frustrated, she asks, "Well, how do you learn if you're not open to feedback?"

I say, "I learned a long time ago that when someone judges you, giving them space to project that judgment only takes away their responsibility for reflection. I have also seen that feedback from a person who is not reflecting on themselves tends to be filled with the idea that I should be different.

"There is a possibility of us exchanging feedback. That is by answering the question, 'How did I make you feel?' If you'd like to share that, then I have the entire day. But I'm not open to you dropping off your discomfort in the guise of 'feedback.'"

Her frustration rises visibly. "Well, if that's the way you live," she says, "you'll never have the opportunity to learn from others. You'll only surround yourself with people who validate your reality."

I say, "In your perspective that may be true. But keep in mind, why would I want to spend any time with someone who is judging me? Why would I spend my time with anyone who is not looking at me with love and compassion? I love feedback. I just don't need to spend my time with people whose 'feedback' says more about them than about me."

She retorts, "You are not open."

I reply, "Fuck you. Fuck you and your judgment. You go through life judging others as if you have some superiority. All the while not sharing anything of yourself. Shutting others down so that you can feel less uncomfortable. I am not interested in participating, thank you."

"You are triggered," she says.

"Yes, I am. How would you feel if you were being judged to your face? I am allowing myself to look at you in the face and say, 'Fuck you for judging me.' That's freedom. I don't have to take your judgment and pretend like it's not there."

She looks puzzled. I don't display any of the training on how people are "supposed to" respond. Instead of continuing down this path, I take the moment to flip it on its head. I look in her eyes and show the vulnerability she is unwilling to show me. With tears in my eyes I say, "It is not easy to allow myself to be freely myself while facing judgment from others. As you separate from your emotions, there is a cost to the people around you. I am showing you that cost.

"I am being authentic. I know that being so will also come at a cost. Some people will not be able to see me. I don't ask them to be different. I don't judge them for judging me. I am allowing myself to be fully me. You're allowed to be you. We can decide if we belong together. Or even if we want any further contact.

"But what I won't do is sit here and pretend that you're not judging me. That would be inauthentic. I have spent years with that inauthenticity and I don't have time for it any more."

I can see she is still perplexed. But at the same time, she sees me. It seems she needed to see me before she could trust me.

We laugh. We then speak openly for the next half hour, seeing one another, feeling closer, appreciating the different ways we live. By the time our conversation ends, she jumps off of the bench and asks, "Can we hug?" We hug and I feel a deep connection, the kind of connection that arises when you are able to love yourself and the other in equal measure.

CHAPTER 14

He Loves Me, He Loves Me Not

(Big Sur, California)

On my last day at Esalen, I say goodbye to the group. My friend's soon-to-be ex-wife is there. I have assumed that, since the divorce is coming, she will not want to be around him. But she is still holding out hope and wants to be near him, as if being close will somehow change his mind.

He has told her that he met another woman. Although they have not crossed any lines, he feels a closeness with this other woman that he has not felt with his wife. This is emotionally crushing for her and she is deeply hurt.

Esalen is famous for its hot springs perched on a cliff overlooking the Pacific Ocean. I ask if we can talk there. It's one of the most beautiful places I have ever been. It is a magical atmosphere to connect with the emotions of this intense moment.

We sit in the hot springs bath and I ask, "How are you doing?"

"Strange," she says. "It sucks."

I can see she is holding back deep emotions. Not unlike myself, she uses language as a means of separating from her emotions. I have done it for so many years that it's easy to see in others.

"How are you processing the loss?" I ask.

She says, "I am still in love with him. I believe he'll come around and see that we're meant to be together." She tells me that she left her prior relationship and even her country to move to be with him. "I knew from the moment I met him that we were meant to be together," she says.

More than mourning the loss of her husband, she is mourning the loss of the idea that she carried about their relationship. "We are meant to be together" had become an addictive thought for her. If that's true, the only question pressing on her mind is, "How can I get him to see it?" It reminds me of how the questions we ask ourselves determine how we process the world. Better questions mean better outcomes.

I can see her pain. She is trying to make sense of something that makes no sense. I ask, "How willing are you to share some intensity?"

She smirks and says, "Andy, I don't know how much more intense you can be. My whole life is intense."

I smile and say, "Well, let's give it a try. Are you willing to say something that may hurt, as a way of healing?"

She says, "I am open to anything."

I ask, "What is the hardest thing for you to say?"

"My husband loves another woman."

"Do me a favor and say, 'My husband loves another woman, and it's okay. Actually, it's great.'"

"I can't be okay with the fact that he loves another woman," she says.

"I know you can't, yet I am going to ask you to give it a try. 'My husband loves another woman and it's okay."

She struggles. "Andy, how can I say that it's great, or even okay? It's not okay."

We wait a moment as I see her building up the strength, as if she is about to do a bungee jump.

"My husband loves another woman and it's okay," she says calmly and quietly, observing herself as the words come out of her mouth.

I ask her to repeat it three or four times, which she does. "My husband loves another woman, and it's okay. My husband loves another woman, and it's okay. My husband loves another woman, and it's okay." Tears stream down her face.

I can see she is beginning to touch the depths of her pain. We are no longer talking about it, but are now sharing it. I have noticed in my work that people talk so much about their emotions that it often becomes hard, if not impossible, to get back to the original emotion. It becomes a mental concept, numbed by words. Something we can point to without actually feeling.

With this exercise, we are now really looking one another in the eye. We are together. Our talk becomes less of an effort to solve something and more of an opportunity to share the pain.

I ask, "What is coming up for you now?"

She recounts her own childhood and how unhappy her mother was with her father. "My mother suffered for years," she says, "because my dad wasn't there for her emotionally."

I ask if we can take another step. She replies, "Yes."

I hear the unspoken judgment she has for her mother and I ask her if she will be open to the possibility of letting that go as well. "I am with an emotionally incapable man, and it's okay." She repeats it several times as the tears continue streaming down her face. Her entire body softens as she is making peace with this reality.

I ask her if she is willing to take one more step. "What more could we do?" she asks.

"A lot," I say with a grin. I invite her to say, "I am just like my mother, and it's great. I married a man just like my father, and it's great."

"Now you are pushing it," she says.

"Let's see if we can make some space for that," I reply.

Then she begins. "I am just like my mother, and it's great. I married a man just like my father, and it's great." She is calm and open. As she speaks, I see less and less struggle. She laughs as she reflects on all the ways she has become her mother. She says, "I spent all those years judging her for staying with my father. And now I am in the same situation."

"How do you feel towards your mother now?" I ask.

She says, "I have a lot of compassion for her. She clearly did not know how to deal with the situation." She pauses, then says, "Isn't it crazy how we repeat the patterns of our parents?"

"Their example gives us our frame of reference for life," I agree. Moving back to her husband, I say, "Apparently, you screwed up when you married this man."

She has become adept at the self-acceptance practice. She takes a deep breath and jumps right in. "I screwed up marrying this man and it's great."

I ask her to say, "My husband never loved me."

She says calmly, "I am not triggered by that because I know he loved me. It's just that we are not in love." She explores what is true for her. She takes a deep breath and exhales. "My husband has never seen me, and it's okay."

As we go through the process, more and more issues come to the surface. "My self-worth has come from my relationship with this successful man, and it's okay. I don't know how I will be self-confident without him, and it's okay. I am valueless without my husband, and it's okay."

As she begins to relax and embrace all these things without judgment or emotional baggage, I see a calm overcome her. She is no longer triggered by these aspects of her life, which she has resisted for so long.

What I have seen is that emotional tension is heightened to the degree to which we are unable to fully embrace it. I like to use the word "grounding" to explain how it works in me. It's like electricity that needs to touch the ground in order to dissipate. If it does touch the ground, it remains as latent energy in the air. Fully embracing an emotion, especially one we're avoiding, is grounding that energy. Giving it a place.

She sits in a state of wonder. I ask her to say, "I am valueless without my husband and it's great. I am nothing without my husband, and it's great." She repeats it alongside me looking over the Pacific Ocean with a calm comfort.

As we let go of all of these ideas she is suffering around, I ask her, "Can we try the next experiment?"

"Yes," she quickly replies.

"I'd like you to now say, 'I am valuable, regardless of whether or not I am with my husband.'"

She repeats this statement over and over again, as if she is reacquainting herself with the power that has always been there. I then ask her to say, "My mother was stronger than I ever could have imagined, whether I am able to see it or not."

We spend the next half hour embracing all of her strengths. Now that she does not resist any idea about herself (i.e., not wanting to be something), she begins to feel the peace that arises when you're okay with everything because you're not judging what you should or should not be.

CHAPTER 15

Learning to Take Care of Me

(Santa Barbara, California)

By the time I reach Santa Barbara, I am already 2,000 miles into my journey. I am beginning to feel the physical and emotional toll on my body.

I'm here to visit Darya, a high school friend with whom I've had very little contact since graduation, thirty years ago. Darya is a holistic health practitioner. She has arranged two sessions for the groups she is working with.

After completing the two sessions, I have one day left with Darya. She is incredibly giving. She doesn't only want me to give my gifts, but she wants to show and give her gifts to me. I recognize that this is hard for me to accept. It's always been easier for me to give love than to receive it.

Darya's first gift to me is a two-and-a-half-hour massage. She works through my body and feels into all the areas where I am holding pain and tension. She immediately recognizes tension in my lower back, which has been hurting for a while.

She can feel that my breath is shallow. She instructs me to deepen my breaths into my stomach to feel my core, and to feel the ground underneath my feet. She explains, "You're going to be absorbing the emotions of others. So you'll need to give that emotion a place."

I have also had trouble digesting food. My diet has changed since I started the trip and my stomach doesn't appreciate it. I also see I have a hard time relaxing into the emotional strain I feel in my lower abdomen. As I breathe deeply into my stomach, I feel a settling.

After my massage, I begin to share with Darya my own practices of release. She reveals struggles with her family she's dealing with. She feels frustrated that her family isn't closer than it is. They've had a lot of drama in the past, and she hasn't been able to reconcile it. One of the relationships she struggles with most is with her twin brother. Every time I mention his name, she is triggered.

Although I'm not judging him, she immediately turns defensive and say things like, "Yes, but he's not that bad a guy." Or, "He also does great things." I hear in this defensiveness a need to reconcile her own emotions around him.

I ask her to embrace the thing that is hardest for her to say. In this case, it is, "I hate my brother, and it's okay." I can see the tension in her eyes as I ask her to repeat it.

"But I don't hate my brother," she says.

I reply, "I understand you don't hate him. But I also see that, by not embracing the fact that this emotion is there, you're fighting against it all the time. And although you don't constantly hate him, there are certain emotions that come up that resemble hatred. So instead of fighting them, I invite you to just to embrace it."

Finally, she is able to utter the words, "I hate my brother and it's okay. I hate my brother and it's okay. I hate my brother and it's wonderful."

Slowly but surely she begins to laugh. She is puzzled. "I see that it feels different," she says, "although it is hard to give it words." She then shares, "I am so sad that my family isn't able to connect the way I want them to."

"Okay, let's have another go at it," I say. "My family is dysfunctional and it's okay. My family isn't capable of feeling my love and it's okay. I suffer because I am not able to have the family I want, and it's okay." She reclaims these unresolved aspects of herself, one after the other.

Then, we complement her acceptance with the opposite: "I love my brother whether I hate him or not. I love my brother regardless of the feelings I have toward him. My family is perfect, whether I can see it or not. I am loved by my family regardless of how I feel."

In the end, Darya says, "Andy, our work is very similar. I feel people's physical states, and I help them by massaging out strained areas. The first time you massage the strain, it hurts like hell. My work is to support people through the initial pain so that they can feel the release.

"Your work is no different. When you ask me to feel the depth of the pain, you're really asking me to 'massage' my pent-up emotions until it stops hurting. And when you first start massaging, it's always going to hurt because the emotional 'muscles' have tightened around the pain. So you have given me some pain, but also the comfort that comes from breaking through it."

She thanks me and I thank her in return. I experience through Darya that there is profound beauty in leaving yourself vulnerable to another, letting them take care of you. Letting them guide you, as you guide others. She teaches me that the weight of the world isn't on my shoulders. I am just carrying my own weight and allowing other people to shoulder their own. She makes my load lighter.

One of the last pieces of advice Darya gives me is that I should drink a lot more water. I take her advice as I travel to my next destination, Santa Monica. I promise to take care of my health from this moment forward. I go to the local CVS and purchase twenty-four bottles and store them behind the driver's seat.

As I drive down the Pacific Coast Highway, I drink bottle after bottle of water—much more than I normally consume. It's not long before I have to go to the bathroom. Seriously. There are very few parking spots along the PCH. According to Google Maps, I have a half hour to my next destination. I know that I am not going to make that so I keep an eye out for a place to stop.

I know a place I could stop, but it's blocked by construction. I then see a gas station, but it's also blocked off. I keep driving, desperate for a place to stop. I keep holding, thinking I'll find something at the next light. As I near Santa Monica, the traffic starts to gather and I am building up to a disaster.

Minutes turn into an eternity. Every place I turn, I can't find a place to stop. Eventually, the pressure becomes too much. I pee myself in the seat of my Toyota Corolla. The puddle sinks into the seat beneath me.

The only thing I can do is laugh at the absurdity of the situation. How did I get to this point? I decided before this trip to surrender to everything that happens, and this is my current reality.

I finally arrive at my destination in Santa Monica. I park behind the house where I am staying, take off all my clothes, and put on a new set. I spend the next hour cleaning the seat. I keep thinking to myself, *This car is going to stink like pee my entire trip.*

The thought makes me laugh. Something I once would have been ashamed of is now something to be celebrated. I tell everyone I meet, from the cashier to the people I stay with, and laugh together with them. I realize that it's often the shame that holds us back from loving everything as it is.

Me and my Toyota traveling across the USA.
Esalen, California

My 10,000–mile route through America.

Advertisement from my first misfired session.
Seattle, Washington

Squeezing everything into the trunk.
Portland, Oregon

Walking to see Kurt Cobain's memorial bench.
Seattle, Washington

Surprise session at the Vietnamese retirement community.
Seattle, Washington

Passing through the destruction of the fires.
McArthur, California

FOX 2
KTVU

AUTHOR TRAVELING THE COUNTRY ASKING
WHO WOULD YOU WRITE A LAST LETTER TO?

Finding my pants and making my way to the morning show.
Oakland, California

Visiting magician and research scientist Kim Silverman with Alton.
Cupertino, California

The Old Capital Books bookstore.
Monterey, California

The view from the hot baths at Esalen Institute.
Big Sur, California

My friend and healer, Darya.
Santa Barbara, California

Signing and dropping a book off at Oprah's house.
Montecito, California

The memorial at the session with my family.
West Hills, California

A photo of Rocky as she cares for one of the many children at the orphanage.
Nairobi, Kenya

The moment I remembered being told about my mother's death.
Irvine, California

CHAPTER 16

A Session With My Brother

(West Hills, California CA)

It is a beautiful Sunday afternoon in Los Angeles. I am at my brother Danny's house, about twenty minutes away from where I was raised, where I will be holding a session. It's a strange feeling, coming back. Everything is familiar, yet it has all changed.

In my stomach, I know this session will be unlike any other, although I'm not sure how. What I'm certain of is that sharing the story with my family, the ones who suffered the same loss as I did, is not going to be easy. We haven't spoken much about it over the past thirty years, but now we are going to dedicate an entire afternoon to the subject.

At my brother's house, the thing that catches my eye most

is a shrine of pictures and remembrances from our childhood. They are all set out on the table, as if it is a wake. In some ways, it feels like I am living the funeral service all over again. Only this time, I am living the same experience with all the emotion I've held down for all these years.

A sense of dread comes over me. I cannot anticipate how hard it will be to relive these emotions in front of the people who have suffered as I have. A few weeks earlier as we planned the session, my sister-in-law had asked, "Is it possible to make this session a little less emotional?"

I said, "I can't promise that, but I wouldn't invite anyone you are worried to be emotional in front of." Inside, I thought, *I don't know how to make it less emotional, because allowing my emotions is the intention of the entire trip.*

We spoke for some time about who she was planning to invite. In the end, nothing was decided, so I arrive not knowing what to expect. When I arrive, I ask my brother, "Who will be coming?"

He informs me that it will be one of my mother's best friends, Zanda, and her husband Bob, as well as their son, Jason, one of my best friends from grade school. Zanda and Bob were the ones who drove to tell Danny, "Your mother died in an accident last night."

On hearing this, a wave of emotions washes over me. I have not seen them since my mother's death. I am not even sure how I'll begin. I've hidden my emotions from them for so long that baring them now is daunting. The same pain I was afraid to share then arises again now.

I begin the session, sharing my gratitude that everyone has come, and my feelings of helplessness as I look in the eyes of everyone.

"I am at a bit of a loss," I begin. "I see that whatever I share is not new to you, since we have all lived the same experience.

Instead of me telling you the story, I'd like to share how the healing process has been for me."

As I speak, I feel my throat constrict as it always does when I feel intense emotions. It feels as if I am choking on my words. Tears are streaming down my face. I make it halfway through a sentence and I feel my body protesting. I slow myself down. I look in the eyes of each person there. Instead of telling everyone, I allow them to see me. Words are too confining.

The most difficult person to look at is my childhood friend, Jason. I see him holding an immense pain inside of him as I speak. His face looks almost contorted. I recognize the look from my past. It is incredibly difficult to look into his eyes and recognize myself in his expression.

At the same time, I realize that all the pain I've bottled up for so many years is also a byproduct of my environment. It is exactly the face I see in Jason that I do not want to create. I do not want to make people feel uncomfortable or add to their emotional burden.

What I am learning through this trip is that the opposite is actually true. When I am able to share my emotion, without judgment, I am able to support others in their emotional development. It is the chicken and the egg conundrum. Which comes first? Do I share my emotions? Or do I blame the world for not showing theirs and then hide mine as a result?

In that moment, I am confronted with everything I've been holding back for so many years. Without stopping or trying to apologize, I embrace my tears. I share with everyone, "I often cry during these sessions." I laugh as the tears stream down my face. I look at my sister-in-law and say, "I guess this is going to be an emotional session."

I add, "For the majority of my life, I have suppressed the feelings around Mom and her death. This will not be one of those moments."

I share my personal stories, the ones that hit me hardest. Then something quite remarkable happens. The session shifts away from my experience and each person begins to share their own. Bob says, "Going to the dorm room to tell you that your mother died was the hardest thing I have ever had to do."

Zanda shares, "On that day I lost a best friend. I don't feel that I have ever recovered."

My brother shares his struggle concerning the woman who killed my mother and how she was prosecuted. The district attorney did not want to try the case because there were no eyewitnesses. At the time, Danny researched the traffic light where the accident occurred and found everything that pointed to guilt. The district attorney finally relented.

I am witnessing firsthand what happens when you don't protect, but rather allow yourself to be seen. I've spent years hiding this part of me and now I am seeing how life could be if I allow it.

We end up speaking for so long that I begin to wonder if we are going to end up writing letters. I ask the group, "Would you still be open to giving this practice a shot?"

I give a quick explanation and we all agree. We spend the next thirty minutes writing, in silence. As we sit, I feel a deep connection to my dad. I've felt that in many ways, my mom has been amplified, while Dad has been relegated to a lesser position. I use the time to write him a letter.

When we come back together, I feel a quiet beauty. We have all shared such a powerful time together that there is a spaciousness in the room. Bob hands me a letter that he's written to his brother, who took his own life after a battle with terminal cancer. Bob whispers, "Can you imagine the strength he must have had to end life on his own terms?"

Stacey, my sister-in-law, hands me a letter she has written to me. "It's not easy for me to be vulnerable," she says. "I am grateful that you did all this. It gave me the strength to be vulnerable."

I realize that for so long, I used others as an excuse for my own inability to be vulnerable. All the people who are sharing this intimacy are exactly the ones whom I have blamed for years. I learn an important lesson. It is not that they were not there for me, but that I was not there for myself.

I am reveling in one of life's ironies. By being totally vulnerable, without the need or expectation that we will be met with the same, you will often be met by others in that space. For all those years when I was suffering and needing it most, I had not been giving space for anyone to meet me.

CHAPTER 17

Visiting Mom and Gina

(San Fernando Mission, California)

After the session with my brother, I drive to San Fernando Valley, where I was raised. On the way, I remember that somewhere along this freeway is the cemetery where my mother is buried. I don't pull over immediately, but rather watch exit signs to see if anything catches my attention. Then I see the San Fernando Mission exit. My stomach drops as I remember going to the cemetery almost thirty years ago.

It feels like fate is bringing me here. I turn off the freeway, pull over, and open Google Maps. Sure enough, the entrance to the cemetery is close by. As I drive through the gates, it feels surreal—just as the experience of my mother's death felt surreal.

It takes me just minutes to find my mom's grave. Everything

I have avoided for all these years is lying right in front of me. The headstone is weathered and grass has grown over the sides. I grab a water bottle from the car and use it to clean the dirt off the headstone.

As I stand looking at her grave, I struggle to let the emotion in. Even though I have spent so much time sharing the pain in sessions, standing back in this moment isn't easy. I am opening a traumatic part of my past, and the patterns from that moment are still connected to it. Namely, when I feel emotions, I turn them into thoughts, instead of just feelings.

I feel the tears come up, but they are just a fraction of the emotion underneath them. I realize I need to sit quietly. Pushing the experience too quickly prevents the emotions from coming up naturally. Words start to come up. "Mom, I have missed you. For many years I was lost without you. I know that you are guiding me now."

Speaking these words, I feel the pain of the past. Speaking to her directly makes it real. I am not thinking about her. Instead, I am with her. I feel a deep well of tears come up, the pain I've suppressed for all those years. I sit and clean the headstone, knowing it is nothing more than a symbol for someone who once existed. Yet at this moment, it is more than enough.

I sit for the next few minutes, recalling memories as they stream back in. I see the birthdays, the days when she'd be crying after arguing with my father, the happiness she felt while making Christmas decorations. I hold the memories with love.

As I stand up to walk back to the car, I remember that a dear friend from high school, Gina, is buried close to my mother. Gina was a bubbly, loving friend who died from stomach cancer soon after my mother was killed. We spoke on the phone a few times before her death. Her voice was weak and it was hard to share anything without feeling that it was all so insignificant. I just told her I loved her and I was going to miss her.

Mom and Gina were close, so it is fitting that their final resting places are close to each other. I have often thought that I could have died in the place of Gina. I've been lucky to enjoy an additional thirty years to live. I have always been grateful for that time, knowing how quickly it can disappear.

While leaving, I ponder on a question that arises. What is the balance between looking into the past and bringing up the pain, and just moving on and leaving the past behind? I have seen people stay in a perpetual state of wishing for a moment in the past to return. In the past, I have judged this as futile, as if two lives were lost in that moment—the one who died and the one who couldn't let go.

In this moment, the question feels like it is being answered. When I ran away from the loss of my mother, I was avoiding the pain. I was searching for peace by way of activity. Now, I am bringing the past to give it a place today. I am not managing the emotions, as I have for so many years, either through denial or escapism.

I see clearly that it is not about managing the emotion, but rather embracing it. Loving it. Knowing that every memory is a gift. Every tear a sign of love for a woman who shaped so much of my life. In many ways, my feelings haven't changed, but my experiences of those feelings have.

I say to myself out loud, "I am a sad and emotionally incapable imposter, and it's okay." I smile, knowing I have moved beyond the captivity of that statement. I am no longer wallowing in the pain. I am giving it a place. I am welcoming it and cherishing it. It is part of my past and apparently, part of my present. I am going to turn fifty and I have never gotten over my mother's death. *And it's okay.*

CHAPTER 18

"I Am Just Like My Mother."

(Saugus, California)

I drive to Saugus to meet an old high school friend, Rocky. I had reconnected with Rocky two years earlier on a chance meeting in Amsterdam. She shared with me a project in Kenya she was working on.

While on her trip to Kenya, Rocky had visited an orphanage where she discovered that the priest running the orphanage was sexually molesting the children. Instead of doing what most of us do, raise our hands and ask, "What can I do?" Rocky decided to do whatever she could to get the children out of that situation. She started by renting a location to house the children. Ten years later, she was responsible for feeding and clothing more than fifty children in a building complex into which she poured her life to support.

I was in awe. It was one of those stories that make you question what contributions you have made in this life. What risks you have taken. It got me thinking: *What am I not doing because it isn't convenient? Where am I comfortably drifting?* Inspired by Rocky, I began thinking less about how I wanted to live, and more about how I wanted to die. What in my life is worth dying for? I imagined my funeral service and thought, *What will they say? How will I be remembered?*

Those questions inspired this trip. When *The Last Letter* was well-received, I followed the impulse to take this journey. I had no idea how I'd achieve this or even if it was possible. I just knew that I was going to do it. I was dedicating myself to something greater than myself.

Rocky taught me that to act is more important than to rationalize why you are not acting. I am missing this urgency in myself. I see how thoughtful I have become, and in that thoughtfulness, I have lived with a sense of complacency.

Visiting Rocky is a time to celebrate what she has inspired in me through her selfless action. I see in Rocky something that I am beginning to discover in myself. Fear and uncertainty are no longer guiding me. A clarity of purpose has taken its place. It is a time to cherish Rocky, and myself, for doing the thing that isn't easy. It is my opportunity to pay off an unspoken debt.

Rocky and I have a few hours to spend together before we begin our session. We find a local sushi restaurant where we catch up with each other. The last time we spoke, she shared the tension that she was experiencing with her mother, which she had felt since our childhood. "My mother is so difficult," she says. "She's self-absorbed and hard to deal with. I'm not interested in having any contact with her. I don't need her energy in my life."

I understand. I learned early in my coaching practice that there is no use discussing a topic that is already so clear. It tends to create frustration. So I handle it lightly.

"How is it for you?" I ask.

She says, "I am sad about it, but I don't have an alternative."

I say, "What happens when you are with her?"

"Well, it always ends in a fight. She tells me what I am doing wrong and I react to it."

She then goes into several stories. I can see she is creating a caricature of her mom. I know it because I have done the same to my father. I've shared the same stories over and over again so that I could crystallize a picture of him. This helped me justify all the reasons we were not speaking.

Although I sense this, I don't share it. I learned long ago that trying to help someone before they have a question is wasted energy.

She continues sharing and I ask, "Would you consider writing your last letter to her?"

She winces. "I don't believe I am ready for that yet."

"Yes, I can imagine."

We spend the next hours talking about everything under the sun. But I am well aware that the invitation to rethink how she is in relation to her mother has set off an avalanche in her brain.

We come back to the subject and she asks, "How were you able to make peace with your father? He did so many terrible things. What changed?"

I say, "For years I did not really see him. I knew how he made me feel and I blamed him for that. I didn't allow myself to see him for who he was, to just let him in. I didn't know how to say no to him without it being a defensive reaction to him."

She nods. "I guess I have not really done that either. And I'm not sure I'm ready for that yet."

I say, "Understandable. Somehow when it's a parent, we feel as if we can't say no. What I've learned is that if I am comfortable holding a 'No' with love, I can let just about anyone in."

"What is a 'no' with love?'"

"That's when I say no to a situation, not the person. For instance, 'I love you, but I can't let you do that.' Or, 'I know this is important to you, but it cannot happen that way.' If you are comfortable with loving, and at the same time not self-sacrificing, it's easier to let people in."

"To do that, I would need some compassion for my mother."

"Yes, that would help," I respond. "But even more important than compassion for her, I'd consider compassion for yourself."

"What do you mean?"

"Well, if you look at all the things that you judge in your mother, I think you'll find that you have those same traits as well. I can imagine that you judge those parts of yourself."

She has not anticipated this direction, and it's obvious on her face.

I ask, "How would it be for you to say, 'I am just like my mother, and it's okay.'"

"No, you're not going to get me to say that," she protests.

I smile and say, "You know me well enough to understand that I am going to get you to say it at some point or another. So why not save us both the effort?"

She says it. Not once, but many times. I watch her soften. At first, it is all rational. Then it turns to a loving voice. Her body relaxes. She says, "Yeah, I can feel that."

A few weeks later, Rocky calls to inform me that she's met her mother for the first time in years. She tells me that it was a wholly different experience. "It was weird. I wasn't charged. I just felt sorry for her. I never realized how stuck she was."

She thanks me and we have a laugh together. We both appreciate how wonderful life becomes when you don't spend all your time letting it be consumed by others. We just need to accept that we are just like them.

CHAPTER 19

The Track Field

(Irvine, California)

*A*fter a session with Rocky, I drive to Irvine, the home of UC Irvine where I ran track and field as a college student. I was practicing on that field when my brother came to tell me that our mom had been killed by a drunk driver, which I wrote about in *The Last Letter*.

I drive to the college, and park near the field. I walk onto the field and am flooded with memories. The long jump pit where I spent much of my time is no longer there and has been moved to the other side.

As I walk across the field reminiscing, I pull out my phone thinking that it will be a nice moment to post something on social media. I record, "I'm visiting the field where I spent much of my time in college. It's also significant because it's where I was informed about my mother's death."

As I hear the words come out of my mouth, I shoot back to the moment. I am not thinking about it, but looking with the same eyes that I had then. I feel the moment. The pain. The loss. The overwhelm.

I cut the recording and begin to sob. I walk to a shelter nearby, sit down, and cry.

After my emotions have settled, I walk to the exact spot where my brother delivered the news. I look around and little has changed, except for me. I am looking at the same pain from the same location, with thirty years in between.

The memory feels as if it is in my body. Hidden in a deep, dark hole that needs light. The tears stream as I walk the same walk now that I did with my brother to his beat-up Fiat. I wipe the tears from my face as I come to the parking lot. I feel so alive.

I walk across the campus to the library. The librarian tells me that there is a special collection for books written by the school's alumni. I pick up one of my books from my car and drop it off there, once again embracing my new status as an author.

There is one last thing to do, which is to have dinner with my dear friend and mentor, Dr. Raymond Novaco. Ray was my philosophy professor in college.

I meet Ray and his wife at an Italian restaurant on Balboa Island. They have been here often and the owner comes to greet us as we walk in. I have brought a copy of the book. His wife is a New Zealander by birth and we share a sense of humor that makes it comfortable to be together.

At the dinner table I ask if I can read a portion of the book where I mention him. They both welcome it. I read:

I have tended to find people to replace the love I wished to receive from my father. Ray was the first male figure in my life to fill this need. I was unaware of it at the time, but I needed the masculine energy of a father, without the anger. In this relationship, I discovered that it was possible to develop a respect, and at the same time, love. There are times in life when you need someone to give you the confidence you cannot give yourself. One of the most incredible moments of my life is when I went back to visit the school to see Ray with his students and he said, "I'd like to introduce you to one of the best students I have ever had." To this day, it brings tears to my eyes.

My eyes water as I read this to Ray and his wife. I am baring my soul to a man who had given me an incredible opportunity to restart life. He reaches out and touches my hand, acknowledging the beauty of the moment.

CHAPTER 20

Finding Peace in Las Vegas

(Las Vegas, Nevada)

I leave Irvine the next day and head east. I stop in Las Vegas and look on my phone for last-minute hotel offers. I see one hotel in the center of the city offering rooms at $25 a night. It is the cheapest by far, and the reviews show four out of five stars.

I confirm the hotel with a swipe of my finger and drive there. It's near Fremont Street, the older part of Vegas that has been revitalized. After settling into my hotel room, I walk out onto the streets, where I encounter all forms of strangeness. One woman walks past me with two stickers over her nipples. I walk around an elderly man wearing a G-string and playing a guitar. People gather around him, pointing and gawking. There are women dressed up in scanty outfits, asking tourists to take pictures for payment.

I've spent the first month of my journey connecting with my emotions and slowing down. I've had little time for TV or other outside stimulation. Now I find myself in an environment that is completely overwhelming. Everything is screaming for my attention. Everything needs to be even more drastically absurd in order to draw more and more attention to itself.

What hits me is that, in order to survive the onslaught of stimulus, I begin to emotionally shut down. I look straight ahead instead of side to side, and avoid making eye contact. I walk deliberately. I do everything to protect myself.

I feel a sense of numbness come over me. The softness and subtlety of life is lost in the midst of all of the emotional shutdown around me. I see this environment as a metaphor for all of society. The contrived street to create a sense of community. The street actors playing their parts as entertainment for the masses, as they point and laugh at the shamelessness of each other. Everyone is playing their role under the canopy of this circus tent.

We often get lost in the endless stimuli of modern life, which is nearly impossible to shut out. We are unaware that we have lost connection. I see people going to yoga and meditative practices to compensate for it. Even separating themselves by moving away from cities.

For empathic people like me, blocking out the stimulus is that much harder. Yet finding a way to be at peace with all of this chaos is really the journey I am on at the moment. I want to be in touch with my emotions, regardless of where I am. I do not want to find places where I can be peaceful. Rather, I want to find peace inside myself, no matter where I am.

I allow my emotions to settle and look back out on the street. I begin to feel compassion for everything and everyone. I see the alcoholic looking for his next drink. The scantily-clad woman trying to get money to pay the rent. The tourist looking to escape his otherwise boring life. It all makes sense.

I recognize that this world does not pull me closer to my emotional center. It actually takes me farther away. But by the same token, I can also see how attractive this world could become. If you shut down your emotions, as most of us do, it's exactly in this world of stimulation where one feels alive again. It's exactly this world that gives you that short hit of excitement. Living on the edge without going over it.

When I left the US twenty-eight years ago to travel the world, I needed places just like this. This was the high I was looking for. Now it just drains my energy. There is nothing I need from it. I am filling my hole from within.

My wife has often told me that traveling gives her something to look forward to. She is motivated at the office if she has something in the future she is working towards. I have always laughed and said, "What if every day felt that way?"

She always replies, "Yes, but you do not need anything from life."

I've learned that if we look at each day as potentially our last, we make different decisions. We live with urgency, which means we don't get lost in the regrets of yesterday or the fears of tomorrow. We don't suppress our emotions, so we don't need a place like Fremont Street to let them out. Places where people feel unseen in their suffering. Places to hide in public. In my sessions, I'm looking to create the exact opposite. We invite vulnerability without an ulterior agenda. We just sit with love and care.

Fremont Street is a great gift. It reconnects me with my reason for taking this trip to begin with: finding connection in spaces where it feels nearly impossible.

CHAPTER 21

The Native American Hitchhiker

(Flagstaff, Arizona)

My next stop after Las Vegas is Flagstaff, Arizona, where my friend Fred lives. The first time I met Fred, it seemed to me that he was born into the wrong culture. He feels more at home in the Native American community than he does in his own. From his clothing to his decorating, it's clear he loves being close to nature.

I have dinner with Fred and a group of his friends. The next morning, I wake up and wonder what my next stop will be. I have two days to get to Santa Fe, New Mexico and I don't have a planned route. Fred needs to leave for work early and we have a quick coffee.

I ask him, "What route do you suggest that I take?"

Without skipping a beat he says, "If I were you I would go to the Navajo and Hopi reservations. You're never going to have a second opportunity to experience a more unique culture in the United States." He goes on to explain, "The poverty in these areas is greater than anywhere else in the US. More than thirty percent of the people living there don't have running water."

I'm not sure what to expect, but I think it will be a great opportunity to explore a part of the US with which I am wholly unfamiliar. At nine a.m., I leave Flagstaff to head into the unknown.

The first stop is Leupp. It's hard to call it a town—it's more like a row of houses next to the road. Housing is primarily caravans and mobile homes that have structures built around them. Nothing seems permanent. I stop to get gas at the station. It is all a bit surreal. I feel a foreigner. I'm not greeted as I shuffle through the makeshift supermarket. I just get my gas and continue on to my next destination, Kykotsmovi Village.

After driving northward for about twenty minutes, I see something surprising: a man on the side of the road. I haven't seen any signs of civilization since I left Leupp. I have no idea where he came from or how he got there. I pass him, then think, *What an opportunity. I'm driving through the Navajo reservation and now I can share that time with someone from the area.* I stop the car and put it in reverse. He jogs to meet me.

He is in his fifties, well-kept, and holds a cowboy hat in his hand. He is carrying a small backpack. As he comes to the door, I roll down the window and tell him where I'm headed.

"That's not where I'm going," he says. There's a long pause while I watch him thinking.

I say, "Well, I can take you to the next city if that helps."

Another long pause. He stands there quietly and I can't quite grasp if he wants to step into the car or not. After at least ten seconds, I ask, "Would you like to get into the car?"

He still stands there. "You can get in now," I assure him.

Finally, he says, "Yes." It is absent of gratitude.

He sits in the car next to me and we drive. For the first five minutes, he does not say a word. I introduce myself and he just sits there. Then surprisingly, he speaks. "Where are you going?"

I tell him the city and he nods. The next stop is about thirty minutes away, so I presume that we will sit quietly the entire time. Whenever I try to spark up a conversation, there is a long pause. Sometimes I think he does not understand me, but then he responds. "What is your name?" I ask.

He sits quiet for about a minute and then answers, "J.W."

"Those are your initials?"

"Yes, those are initials." No further explanation is offered.

Then he begins to point at things. He points at buffalos and says, "Beef." A few minutes pass and he points to a dry pond. "Rainwater."

We spend the next half hour pointing at things. I point at the beautiful mesa in the distance and he says, "Red rock." I point at the clouds and he says, "White sky." He always pauses before his statements. It dawns on me that his way of seeing the world has a groundedness to it. He is pointing out the essence of everything. Things were not mental concepts, but he saw them in a raw, experiential state.

When I tell him I will be driving until the end of November, J.W. says, "Oh, before the snow." It dawns on me that snow is exactly what distinguishes winter from the other seasons, and speaking about it in terms of snow brings it back to a real experience. Snow is something you can touch. Winter is the concept, a few months on the calendar.

At some point I ask J.W. where he is going. He says he is going to Tuba City, Arizona for a fair. "It is a gathering of Navajo and Hopis from around the country," he says.

"Do you go there often?"

"Every year."

Tuba City is just thirty minutes away. "I'll drive you to the fair," I offer.

He is silent. After a long pause, he nods. I'm not sure he understands. He shows no signs of gratitude, as I would have expected. Then again, it isn't necessary.

"How is the relationship between the Navajo and the Hopis?" I ask.

Two-minute pause. "Fine."

"Are you married?"

Another long pause. "I am married, then divorced. I have two children. I don't speak to my ex-wife." I learn not to ask too many questions.

After riding together for about an hour, we're a few miles away from Tuba City. Unexpectedly, J.W. says, "You can drop me off here."

I am confused. "I can take you to the actual fair," I say.

He is silent again. So I pull over on the side of the road and drop him off at a place similar to the one where I picked him up. *Maybe he gets on and off at whatever point feels right to him. Maybe he has no goal in mind,* I wonder.

CHAPTER 22

Contemplating in Hot Springs Under the Stars

(Crestone, Colorado)

I leave early the next morning to get to my next session at Unity Church in Santa Fe. I have two days to get to Denver. Looking at the map, I see a city, Crestone, located about halfway to Denver. I decide to go there.

I arrive at around six o'clock in the evening. A storm passed through a few days earlier that has left patches of snow. Wild deer run across the dirt road, which feels like the yellow brick road leading to Oz. It runs straight to hot springs. The clouds are bright orange and turn red as the sun sets. I stop to take pictures of the overwhelming color display.

This place has a strange energy, an air of alternative living. When I ask one of the customers at the supermarket how he would describe it, he says, "We are a drinking city with a religious problem." Apparently, this energy is a byproduct of its history. In the early 1980s, a couple granted parcels of land to several religious organizations. Each religion has a few acres of land to separate it from its neighbor. It feels like a religious trade show.

In the middle of all this are the "Hill View Hot Springs." Around the hot springs are structures over a hundred years old, which offer travelers a meager, albeit quaint, place to stay. I am put in a dormitory of a ramshackle old house. There is a piano in the middle of the room, played by one of the guests. Other people grab instruments and it becomes a sing-along. There is no exceptional talent, but the atmosphere is welcoming. There is this sense of community and, from what I gather, many of the people have lived here for months in a row.

I awake at three a.m. and can't go back to sleep. Instead of tossing and turning in bed, I decide to brave the freezing temperature and jog to the hot springs about fifty meters away. It is pitch black. I leave the house and run straight into a deer standing a few feet from the door. It runs off. Bats fly around my head under the black sky. Fireflies twinkle in the night.

I turn on my phone light to guide me. I make my way through the forest to the water and jump in. The spring is made of large natural stones pushed together. I find a shallow part, which allows me to lie on my back and look up at the stars. I'm in complete isolation and silence, staring up at the stars.

I see the Big Dipper and Orion's Belt. I think about how insignificant I am in light of the billions of stars blanketing the sky. *How can I make my life so important when I see how little I am?*

I think about my trip so far and see two very big themes emerging: surrendering and self-love. Surrendering means embracing my reality at any given moment. Since I've been letting go of many of my expectations over years, this has not been overly difficult. Self-love, on the other hand, is a bigger challenge.

My mind turns to the self-acceptance method I use. I feel into this practice and see that, in some ways, it has kept me stuck from moving beyond self-acceptance. For me, self-acceptance means making peace with certain aspects of myself and/or my experience. "I'm sad and it's okay." "I really messed that up, and it's okay."

As I hear myself say these phrases in my head, I feel constricted around saying, "It's okay." It means I am still managing the emotion. I am giving the emotion a place, but I'm also keeping it in check. It feels as if I am convincing myself that it is okay, even if on some level I feel as if it is not.

In the past, I would ask a person to share the thing that was most difficult to say, whatever was hardest to be okay with. For example, "I am not loved by my partner, and it's okay." Or, "My parent does not accept me as I am, and it's okay."

Taking simple statements and making them "okay" pacifies the tension, but it doesn't release it completely. It is another coping mechanism. *How would it feel to completely redefine the thought?*

So instead of saying, "it's okay," I try something stronger: "It's fucking great." So instead of saying, "I hate my parents and it's okay," I take it to the next level and say, "I hate my parents and it's fucking great. It's fantastic. It's wonderful. It's freeing." It creates a strange paradox, but it works. Using the stronger version with the "f-word" somehow gives me a freedom to let go of any ideas I hold about myself. It helps me to *completely* embrace the thing I am resisting. Now, the thing I have resisted gives me joy.

With this stronger addition to the method, I am now no longer managing the emotion. I am no longer pacifying the feeling I'm resisting. I am simply embracing it to the point that it loses its stranglehold over my thinking. I decide that, moving forward, I will no longer manage my thinking with techniques. I am ready to explore another level of self-acceptance. In fact, it is much greater than self-acceptance: self-love.

I have been playing with this all throughout my journey, but now I see the essence of this process. What does life look like if you simply love every part of yourself? If you enjoy the judgment cast upon you by others? If you laugh at every thought that does not serve you? If you decide to see everything that constrains you as "fucking great" and you're free? It's radical to take over a thought that's dominated you and destroy it with one fell swoop. That thought may still come up, but there's no longer a negative reaction to it. There's no longer a need to defend. It disappears as quickly as it came.

By now it's four a.m. I stare at the sky thinking, *I am small and insignificant compared to the vastness of the universe, and it's fucking great. It is absolutely amazing.* Finally, I head back to the dorm. The next morning I wake up refreshed and full of life.

After breakfast, I go to the hot springs again. It has proven to be a fruitful place for contemplation. While I am sitting there, I strike up a conversation with a woman, with whom I share my insights. She smiles and shares this story:

> *A senior monk and a junior monk were traveling together. They came to a river with a strong current. As the monks were preparing to cross the river, they saw a young and beautiful woman also attempting to cross. She asked if they could help her cross to the other side.*
>
> *The monks glanced at one another because they had taken vows not to touch a woman. Then, without a word, the older monk picked up the woman, carried her across the river, placed her gently on the other side, and continued on his journey.*

The younger monk couldn't believe it. After rejoining his companion, he was speechless. Hours passed without a word between them. Finally, the younger monk could contain himself and blurted, "As monks, we are not permitted to touch a woman. How could you then carry that woman across the river?"

The older monk replied, "Brother, I set her down hours ago. Why are you still carrying her?"

It's not enough to accept something as "just okay," because we're still beholden to push back and manage it. When the thought arises, we give it time and effort. By saying it more strongly, we trick our brain into letting go of a thought completely, so that it doesn't define us in any way.

Our brain produces thoughts. Most of the time, we have no ability to control thoughts. Being repressed, they come back over and over again. When we are tired and weak. When we are angry and frustrated. In our dreams. It goes back to the old adage, "Don't think of a pink elephant." The surest way to think of something is to tell yourself not to think it. If you say, "Don't think about how your parents treated you," you are in fact inviting that thought to linger on. It will continue to haunt you in different shapes and forms.

This revelation is not something new. Yet it is completely new for someone who has not seen how essential it is to love the things he has disliked, or even hated in himself, for so long.

Of course, I realize this is only one side of the paradox. Because in saying "I love the thing I hate," I also need to embrace the opposite thought so that I am not defined by any thought. For example, "My parents hated me, and it's fucking great," is only one side. The other would be, "My parents love me, whether I can fully embrace it or not." I have achieved a balance in this practice I haven't felt before.

CHAPTER 23

"I'm Nothing without Him."

(Denver, Colorado)

After my stop in Crestone, I make my way to Denver where I have a session scheduled at a bookstore.

Two women show up, one in her late forties and the other in her mid-eighties. The younger of the two says she came because she wants to share vulnerable contact, which she's been unable to find in her area.

She goes on to share with us some marital challenges. She is fearful to leave her husband because she has become dependent on him through the years. She is a psychiatrist by profession, although she has not practiced in many years.

"Once we met, I gave up on my career," she says. "For the last twenty years, I have only been a homemaker." Her eyes appear as if she is on the verge of tears at any moment.

I smile and say, "It looks like this is going to be different than all my other sessions."

I look at the elderly woman and ask, "Would it be okay if we spent our time digging into her challenges?"

"Yes," she says, smiling, almost as if she is excited at the prospect of peeking into someone else's life.

As the younger woman speaks, it becomes apparent that the issue she is facing is fear. The fear of an uncertain future. The fear of financial loss. The fear of losing the relationship with her children. She is grappling with the overwhelming fear of not knowing who she will be without everything she knows. She is miserable, her misery is familiar to her. As she speaks, tears well up in her eyes. "Divorce is failure, and I do not want to fail."

The longer we sit together, the more apparent it becomes that she has a very fixed idea of how life is "supposed to be." I ask, "How is it to be living in the house?"

She explains, "Although I have lived in the same house as my husband, I have not looked him in the eyes for months. When he comes home, I go to a separate room. And when we are in the same room, I avert all eye contact. We have kept in contact through email for the last month."

I ask, "What is wrong with the marriage?"

"He is very dominant. Ever since we were married he was verbally, and sometimes physically, aggressive. I have been bullied for years. I have never had my own voice in our relationship. Whenever I tried, he would only raise his aggression either passively or more overtly. I have learned to be quiet."

I look at the elderly woman and smile. She has mentioned that she has been divorced twice and I ask, "You appear to have a lot of experience in this area. What would you suggest?"

She says, "Leave him."

There is a silence. I say, "Apparently, you have an easier time leaving men."

She replies, "I got fed up with them and left."

This is no help to the younger woman. She is stuck. I ask her again, "What does divorce mean to you?"

She breaks down in tears. "I am scared. I am afraid." She is fearful that her husband will take aggressive action if she proposes to divorce. That idea stops her from even engaging in the conversation. She is deep into a feeling I am very familiar with: self-doubt.

I tell her about my experiences of self-doubt as I was being asked to sign books. The feeling that I didn't deserve to sign them. The feeling that there are better books in the world. I am beginning to see this self-doubt on a wider scale. I tell her that, as a coach, I spend the majority of my time supporting people to overcome self-doubt. "I'm not smart enough." "I'm not educated enough." "I'm not wealthy enough."

There is always a story, often unseen, that is keeping us stuck. Here, I see a woman imprisoned by walls of self-doubt. "I don't know if I am strong enough," she says. She is in tears now and I ask if she'll be open to experimenting with me. She smiles very openly and says, "Of course."

I explain that I am toying with a process of reclaiming emotions. "I'd love to see how your life would feel if you were at peace with some of the things you're struggling with at the moment."

I ask her to say, "I am worthless, and it's great."

She gives me the puzzled look, which I've become familiar with by now. Yet she sees the sincerity in my eyes and says, "I am worthless, and it's great." She repeats it three or four times, each time smiling a bit deeper. Each time feeling more into the relaxation of allowing herself to feel valueless. "How does this work?" she asks.

I say, "Well, if you are blocking something in yourself, maybe something you don't want to admit or gives you shame, then that thing will define you. Your life is a byproduct of that which you resist. So by fully embracing it, even loving it, you take away any power it has over you."

She says in wonder, "Yeah, I see it. I see it."

Then I ask her to take another step and say, "I am nothing without my husband, and it's great." I look to the elderly woman, wondering if she is anxious or triggered. She isn't.

The younger woman pauses a moment and then repeats it over and over again. She cries as she lets the words settle into her system. "I am nothing without my husband, and it's great." We look one another in the eyes and I see a calm overcome her.

In this space, I ask her to take one more step and say, "I am valuable whether anyone recognizes it or not." She sits in her quiet strength for a moment and repeats the words, "I am valuable whether anyone recognizes it or not." She adds, "I am strong. I am not dependent on others for my strength."

As she repeats the words in a soft, grounded voice, it feels as if I am sitting next to a totally different woman. "Wow, it's crazy how that works," she says.

We spend the next hour taking every judgment that comes into her head and reclaiming it. At some point, she starts to laugh hysterically at how she can cut through her own thoughts and no longer be a victim of them.

With that, I close the session. There is no need to write any letters.

CHAPTER 24

My First Stalker

(Boulder, Colorado)

$\mathcal{M}$y next session is at a bookstore in Boulder, about an hour north of Denver. By this time, I've gotten accustomed to very few people showing up at bookstore sessions. Apparently, asking people to be vulnerable in public, with people they don't know, isn't the social norm.

When I arrive at the poetry bookstore in Boulder, my expectations are low. To my surprise, I see the same woman from the night before. She has driven from Denver to Boulder to see me. "I guess I'm your first stalker," she says.

We both laugh. I look around and say, "It looks like we will have the time to ourselves."

"How could it be that no one would show up for this?" she

says. "Oh well, I guess it's no surprise that I am the only one here. Apparently not everybody has a hard time finding people to share vulnerability with."

We sit in the corner of the bookstore and spend the next two hours talking. This time we move a bit faster since she already feels more comfortable with some of the victim roles she carries. I press some buttons on issues where she is holding onto beliefs. She repeats how abusive her husband is. She is unkind and unsympathetic in the portrayal of her husband.

I laugh and say, "You know you've never really appreciated your husband for being aggressive and unsympathetic."

She looks at me with the same puzzled expression she had a day earlier and says, "No, I guess I haven't."

"I am assuming he has always been that way," I say. "I imagine that it's only these last years that you have fully allowed yourself to see it.

"Your resistance to his aggression keeps you stuck in a common pattern that develops in relationships. Each person brings unconscious emotional triggers into the relationship. When our partner triggers us, we react blindly and defensively. We believe we have free will, but we're often just reacting to triggers.

"You have been living the pattern over and over, without any space to break out of it. You've never even had a chance to see him or let him see you completely. You've self-sacrificed for years, and now you blame him for your inability to fully show up as you are."

"You're right," she says. "I have never really allowed myself to be 'me' with him. And I have blamed him for that."

I reply, "Yes, so who are you now?"

She admits that she had suffered so much and is incapable of answering that question. "I don't actually know who I am," she says. She goes on to explain, "I really am just a byproduct of my environment. I allowed myself to be in this for a long time."

"Yes, I can see that. But how does it feel to realize that from this moment forward, you can decide who you want to be? You no longer need to be the woman who self-sacrifices to make other people feel safe and okay."

She takes a deep breath and says, "Yes, I see it. I see it." Then she asks, "How do I make sure to keep this with me after you're gone?"

I laugh and say, "Well, you already know how to do that."

"What do you mean?"

I say, "We have spent the past hours talking about it. Whenever you have a judgment towards yourself, or anyone else for that matter, then there's something there to reclaim.

"For example, 'My husband is loud, and I love it.' 'My husband is a bully, and it's great.' 'I can be loud when I want, and it's great. I am no longer a victim of anyone. You can be loud and I can be loud. I will not avoid you.'"

She uses the practice to move through emotional struggle. Wherever she sees resistance in herself, she moves towards it. "I no longer need to separate myself from others in order to feel a sense of comfort. If I allow myself to actually accept everyone for who they are, without judgment, I can fully allow myself to be whomever I want to be." Then she breathes out. A deep release.

I say, "That's it! As long as you don't blindly follow the critical voice in your head, you are free to redefine how you operate in the world. You are free."

She smiles again and she says, "There's something I want to show you." She pulls out her phone, shows me a picture, and says, "This is a piece of land I'm in love with. It's my husband's. The one thing I want to make sure of when we get divorced is that I get this land." She scrolls through her pictures to show me the land. It is picturesque and gorgeous. She tells me all the things she wants to do with the land.

I say, "What if by being attached to that land, you lost all the freedom you could have to be separated from your husband? Would you rather have that land or the financial freedom that may come as a result of selling it?"

We often get caught in an expectation and attach to it. Once we are attached, it is hard to let go. She has imagined herself living in a house on that land. What she has not yet recognized is that leaving her husband could also mean that this is no longer a reality.

I ask, "How would it be for you if you realized that letting go of everything was all you needed to do to find happiness?"

She smiles through tears, "I know you're right. I guess I just haven't allowed myself the opportunity to let go of this land."

I reply, "You don't need to let go of it. But you certainly do not want to hold onto it from the start. First, let go of it and then see how it plays a role in your life and if it makes sense. At the moment, that land doesn't have any utility. It will cost you more to make it habitable than most people pay for an entire home. It could very well be the next thing that keeps your life in a constant state of suffering.

"If you perpetually need money, where will that leave you? What if the dream of this land was not in living on it, but selling it to live the life of your dreams? How does that feel?"

She smiles.

She is an environmentalist and her husband makes his money through work with Monsanto. I push my luck and jokingly say, "So if Monsanto came to you and offered you a million dollars for that piece of land, it would be incredible. Monsanto would be giving you an opportunity to live the life of your dreams."

She laughs and says, "Now you're really pushing it. No, I would never sell it to Monsanto. But I understand. I will not self-sacrifice. I am going to think about what I need."

With that, we leave the bookstore and she walks me to my car and gives me a big hug. She thanks me and tells me the time we've spent together has changed her life.

CHAPTER 25

Either Abandon Him or Yourself

(Boulder, Colorado)

On my third day in Boulder, a friend invites me to do a session with her friend in the city. Her friend's name is Sharon and she is the minister at a hospital. We arrive at Sharon's house and I have about two hours to get to know her before our session starts. Although she is very open, I sense she needs time to see if I'm the "real deal."

Only women show up at the session. Almost all of them have come directly from the hospital where they work. It's obvious that they meet often and know each other well. Just before starting the session, I hear a woman say, "Just what we need, another man to come into our lives and tell us how we should feel. I have that just about every day."

Little does she know that I'm not coming in to tell her how she should feel, but share how I'm feeling and how I use my feelings to help and support others. The same woman goes on to share in the session, "It took me a while to figure out what you were doing here. As soon as I began to write, I understood exactly. You were inviting me to feel a level of intimacy in myself that wasn't easy. I am grateful."

She writes a letter to anxiety, a feeling she has a hard time accepting in herself. She reads her letter to the group. We all feel where anxiety is touching us. There is no separation in the group. We are all one in that emotion. She creates a connection that moves the group to tears.

I introduce the group to the term "holding space." In some cases, people in the groups will get nervous and defuse the tension with humor. In other cases, the groups can hold the tension in themselves without dropping into coping mechanisms to release it. I also see that when the facilitator of a group is comfortable showing vulnerability, others in a group feel permission to do the same.

In the groups that are able to hold a lot of space, I notice that the people who are struggling most will eventually show themselves. In the face of this incredible embrace of sharing, people feel safe. In the end, it feels effortless.

This is not always the case. Sometimes it is more challenging for participants, even when others are very vulnerable. In these cases, people will often share just a bit of their emotion, and then sit silent until the next person begins. Other times, people will stop once the tears come and say, "I'd like to leave it at that." These are also beautiful moments, but there is no major release of the kind of emotion that often leads to the biggest breakthroughs.

Yet I trust that the space the group can hold is exactly what is necessary for them at this moment. I never push. It is not the space to get anyone anywhere. It is simply a question of how much space we can hold for one another.

In this session, the person having the most struggles is Sharon. She is dealing with many difficult things in the recent past, including divorce and cancer. Vulnerability and intimacy do not come easy to her. She needs time, and possibly fewer people around, to start touching that part of herself again.

The session ends and all the ladies leave, leaving Sharon and me alone. I stay at her house that evening and we watch the Red Sox play the Astros for the division final. Sharon is a huge Red Sox fan. Every time they score, she jumps off the sofa and runs around shouting. Her team wins at the last minute, which sends her into a frenzy, jumping and screaming throughout the house. And I join her.

The next morning, we take her dog out for a walk. I ask her, "What made you so constricted last night?" I can see tension come over her. First, her face freezes. Then her body recoils into itself to hide the pain I'm inviting her to share.

She shares, "I am still recovering. The divorce was not that long ago."

I ask, "Would you be willing to share a bit more?"

She says, "I married a man who could not be there for me emotionally and I am frustrated. I abandoned myself for so long that I couldn't do it any longer."

I ask, "What do you mean, 'abandoned'?"

She explains to me that a friend once told her, "You have one of two choices regarding your husband. You can either abandon yourself or you abandon him."

I think, *There is a third option: abandon neither.* But I let that voice settle, as it will turn me into just another person trying to solve her problems. I don't want to push her away. So instead I follow another track. I share, "I am assuming this behavior is nothing new for you. What's the history behind it?"

She looks confused.

"What is the earliest memory you have of abandoning yourself?" I ask.

"I don't know," she says.

I take the next step. "Where would you have abandoned yourself with either of your parents?"

I see a light of realization turn on in her eyes. "My father was emotionally incapable and he never really understood me. I spent most of my life accommodating him by not being myself, so that he didn't need to feel uncomfortable."

"And where do you see that in your life today?"

She says, "I see it everywhere."

"So what you're telling me is that the behavior that allowed you to survive as a child is still active in you today."

She nods. "Yes, it is still very much who I am today."

I ask her if she'll be willing to investigate further, to which she agrees.

And I say, "I want to make a big assumption and accept it as true for the moment. You are abandoning yourself in every relationship in your life. There is always a way that you are abandoning yourself, whether you see it or not. So we are not asking whether or not you are abandoning yourself, but *how* you are abandoning yourself. Where have you abandoned yourself with me in the short time we've known each other?"

She investigates for a little bit and says, "I don't think I have abandoned myself with you."

I smile and ask, "Well, if you had to guess, where would it be?"

She says, "Well, arranging for the party for people to come, I felt the necessity to make it very special. I wanted to make sure that people felt comfortable and the food was nice. I did abandon myself by imposing on myself that I needed to do well."

I ask, "How would it have been different if you didn't abandon yourself?"

She says, "I would have just invited people, but I wouldn't necessarily have put out a spread and made a very nice dinner for them."

We both laugh. I ask, "What other ways did you abandon yourself?"

She explains, "I did not feel comfortable saying we were going to watch the baseball game after the session. I didn't want to impose that on the group."

I laugh again and ask, "What would it have looked like if you would have imposed it on the group?"

She says, "I would have just said after the session, 'I need to watch the baseball game because I want to see how the Red Sox play.'" She pauses, then smiles and says, "This is so damn easy."

I ask, "How does the pattern play out in other areas of your life?"

"From a very young age, I moderated my behavior when I felt that it was difficult for others to deal with. I assumed others were not interested in what I had to say. So instead of saying it, I would just be quiet. I didn't want to make people feel uncomfortable. I did what I always do: accommodate the other person, or at least my perception of the other person's capacity. In this case, I just assumed people wouldn't want to watch the baseball game and I didn't allow myself to believe that maybe you would enjoy it."

I laugh and ask, "How would your life be different if you just accepted who you were and embraced it and didn't compromise? What if you did not decide what you were going to do, or not do, based on your assumption that the other person may not be capable of accepting it?"

"Yes, I understand that logically," she says. "But I don't do it. I don't know how to shift that behavior."

I say, "There is only one thing needs to happen."

"Tell me."

"You simply say that behavior is no longer acceptable."

"How?"

I reply, "If you don't tell people how you feel, then you perpetuate the behavior you don't want in your life. The only way around it is to say it, from this moment forward. You need to state unequivocally, 'I won't step away and abandon myself when I feel I want something different.'"

She is confused. I go on, "It looks like this: somebody comes to you with a request, or demand, or question of any sort and you don't feel comfortable about it. Instead of doing what you normally do—accommodating it and abandoning yourself—you stay connected to your emotion. If necessary, you say, 'I'll need to reflect on this.' What you don't do is respond immediately from an impulse to please."

Sharon says, "I'd like to use a real example with an employee I'm struggling with. One of the people I work with came to me and asked me to do a task that was actually hers. I was aware that this woman was not fulfilling her role when she came to me at the last moment, and instead of saying no, I said yes. I see that I avoid conflict."

I say, "Yes, none of us want conflict in our lives. But let's assume you're not inviting conflict, but just dealing with an issue. This may cause conflict, but that conflict is not necessarily your responsibility."

"Yes, I understand that."

"This woman has now replaced your father," I continue. "Any time you're with someone who is emotionally incapable, you're accommodating them by avoiding conflict instead of holding them accountable for their behavior. How would you interact with her in a way where you didn't abandon yourself but you're still able to help her take responsibility?"

She says, "I would arrange to talk to her and I would explain to her that in the future this behavior would no longer be acceptable."

I say, "That sounds great. And how do you make sure that you don't create the conflict you don't want?"

She says, "I would tell her what I am feeling, without placing judgment on it."

"Exactly. Instead of blaming her for what she's done, you'd bring forward that this is what's happened so far, and then use that moment to share that that would no longer be acceptable. So it's not acceptable that she brings forward something at the last minute and asks you to do it for her. If you let that happen, you are setting yourself up for a codependent relationship. By allowing her to give up her responsibility, you are basically telling her that this way of working is okay."

She says, "This is something that I have done my entire life. I don't know how to deal with people who are emotionally incapable."

"I gather that. You still are dealing with the same emotions you had as a child. Everyone who is emotionally incapable replaces your father. So what do you do? Self-sacrifice. You bend over backwards to try and make it work. How would your life look different if you just allowed yourself to be who you are, and accept that it will not always work for others?"

She takes a deep breath and says, "It would look a whole lot different."

After a moment of reflective silence, she continues, "I'd like to discuss my marriage and divorce. I spent years feeling like I didn't have a partner. I did not have someone who could comfort me. I needed more. We tried counseling, but it didn't go anywhere. I want somebody to be there for me emotionally. Somebody who can support me when I am feeling uncomfortable. Someone who won't judge my emotions as immature."

She pauses, then continues, "Now that I think of it, I married my father. I needed something from someone who wasn't able to give it. It's frustrating. This is a lesson I have had to learn so many times."

I say, "If someone isn't capable of feeling and sharing their emotions, it does not tend to be their decision. Rather it is their own baggage. Just like your baggage with your father. If I hear you correctly, it appears that you changed in this relationship and now you need more. There is no blame. Just the reality that the relationship is no longer working for you."

"I'm ashamed it has taken me so long to learn this lesson," she says.

I reply, "Instead of judging yourself, wouldn't it be great to celebrate that you actually learned the lesson you needed to learn in order to evolve? Let's celebrate it. In fact, I'd love to use a tool I've been playing with the last few weeks. Could you say, 'I am emotionally incapable, and it's fucking great'? 'I failed in my marriage and it's fucking great'? 'I married my father and it's great'?"

She begins repeating the statements. As she does so, I see her body relax. I can see the self-judgment, which has led her into a vicious cycle of blame and self-doubt, loosen its grip. In place of indecision and discomfort, a new state emerges. She is embracing her shame.

She says, "You look at the world in black and white. You're so open and at the same time so definite. I have always thought that looking at the world in black and white would shut you down. But actually, it's completely counterintuitive."

I say, "Funny, isn't it? The more you see the world as abstract, the less people see you. The more you speak in concepts and less in experiences and feelings, the more people feel a distance. It's safe, but not necessarily emotionally fulfilling. By being present with your experience and treating it totally seriously and at the same time with a lightness, you get to be genuine with others without getting stuck. Once you treat your personal experience as absolute truth, life tends to be an uphill battle."

Sharon goes on to say that it is incredibly difficult for her to be completely authentic, because she is not quite sure how people will react to her if she were to share all of who she is. "You can never be certain how people will react," she says.

I reply, "Yes, that is true. But you also will never know how they'll react unless you are vulnerable. The current situation is that you protect yourself by not sharing, and then you blame the other for not seeing you. You don't even give them a chance."

She asks, "How do I change this in my life?"

I laugh and say, "There is always only one thing you need to change. I mentioned it before. You need to say no every time you recognize you are self-sacrificing. In the moment that somebody asks you to do something and you don't feel good about it, instead of abandoning yourself, you stop. Slow things down. Check in with yourself. Maybe even take a day to think about it."

She asks, "How has this been for you?"

"When I decided to be fully present with who I wanted to be in the world, at first people had a hard time adjusting to what they perceived as a different person. I lost some friends who needed me to be the same as I was before. I tried things that just didn't work, as I was experimenting to see how I could be me without diminishing others.

"I saw that navigating this was not always easy, because people have their own needs and they can be blinded when you don't accommodate their ideas of good and bad. Through the years, I have found ways that work for me.

"And I've also seen a consistency in the patterns that push others away. It comes down to judgment of oneself and others. The more you judge, the more you will tend to get triggered and react to others. Developing this inner compass of consistency is incredibly powerful. The less judgment you have towards yourself and others, the clearer the compass will be in reading its environment. It all starts with letting go of self-judgment."

"It all sounds so simple," she says. "What do you do when

you are confronted with someone who has no desire to see you? Or even judges you?"

I say, "It's funny you ask, as this very thing occurred two weeks ago." I tell her the story of the neuroscientist at Esalen, to whom I said, "Fuck you and your judgment."

Sharon says, "I wish I could do that."

I say, "There's a reason I could behave that way. I learned it by doing tons of other stuff that didn't work. All the books tell you what to do. But my own experience has guided me more than anything, as I have learned to trust it. Books can also create confusion because they create an image of how things 'should be.' People do their best to validate that image, ignoring the signs that it is not working.

"In this instance, I just decided to use the last thing in my arsenal, which may have seemed counterintuitive. When I said, 'Fuck you,' I didn't have any judgment towards that word. It was this display of anger that eventually gave us the chance to be close. In fact, it was in my ability to show anger, without attaching to it, that I had the chance to break through.

"I did not know of this beforehand. It was taking a chance. I can't tell you what to do, but I can tell you what has not worked for me. I learned how important anger is, by seeing that every other way did not work. I don't say I would suggest anger, nor would I discourage its use. I would say be conscious of how your environment is impacted and learn through reflection on that experience."

Sharon ponders my words as we walk back to the house.

As I prepare to leave, Sharon observes, "You are not prepared for the winter." She hands me a coat from her closet and says, "Try it on and take it." I feel love come over me as I see how she is taking care of me. Just as with my time with Darya, I'm seeing how giving is something others feel compelled to return. I am receiving the love I am giving, and it feels beautiful.

CHAPTER 26

Reacquainting Myself with Family

(Des Moines, Iowa)

From Boulder, I make my way east to Des Moines, Iowa, where much of my mom's side of the family lives. I am Mary Kaye's youngest son, and I've come here to reacquaint myself with her family. I'll be staying with my Uncle John, my mother's brother, and his wife, Samantha.

I've never been close with any of the Kaye family. In fact, for years I've felt resentment toward them for not reaching out to me. I blamed them for not being able to give me the emotional support that I sorely needed. Eventually, I saw that it was my inability to ask for help that made it impossible for them to console me. I was so wrapped up in my own loss that I was unable to see that they all lost a sister.

It feels strange. I am having trouble letting go of an old story that has crystallized in my brain. But my intention to surrender and open my heart is stronger.

I arrive at their penthouse overlooking the square in the center of Des Moines. I'm surprised when my uncle dives right into politics. This part of the country is predominantly Republican, which has given me many opportunities to dialogue with the many Trump supporters I meet along the way. Sitting with my uncle is one of these opportunities to dig into the Republican side of things.

He shares his general feelings, "You have to understand that Trump is a New Yorker and you need to look at him in light of that. He says what's on his mind and he does not mind being offensive."

My uncle does not condone the President's behavior, but at the same time, he does not draw any clear boundaries. I'm curious because, since he's the head of a large company, I assume he will have a strong focus on character. But with politics, his primary focus is on policy.

"He is doing things that no recent president has done, namely, fulfilling his campaign promises," he continues. "His focus on deregulation and immigration are making the country stronger." For him, both items are important. He shares this clear-eyed, without emotion. He has given his views great thought.

What I see is that my uncle is so disenchanted with the political system that he has lost faith in politicians. We are actually very similar in that regard. We just choose different ways to deal with these feelings.

As I'm not a supporter of either party, it means I'm always at risk of setting off anyone I speak with. I can hear the words, "You're either with us or against us," being spoken in the quiet recesses of everyone's mind. It often feels less like I am speaking to critical-thinking individuals and more like I am speaking to ideologues.

The political discourse in the US is bewildering to me. I

have long since given up on politics. I have seen that it is based on competition and not cooperation, which means that there is always someone imposing something on someone else. I understand that the system was created to organize society. But my concern is with the lack of compassion the system is based upon. I have experienced it is an "us or them" mentality, which I have seen grow stronger and stronger in the US over the last twenty years.

I respond to my uncle by saying, "I cannot speak to Trump's policies. I just don't find his overall approach to politics appealing."

He replies, "Do you think Hillary would have been any better?"

I learned long ago not to fall into the trap of defending a side. I say, "Just because one side is corrupt does not justify the other to be corrupt."

In the end, we become closer through the talk. I understand his way of looking at the world, and he sees that he is not going to be judged for it. It is a discourse that I was missing for a long time in my visits to the US. Learning from one another, instead of pushing one another away.

That evening we go to dinner, a three-minute walk from the apartment. The restaurant is famous for its duck fat fries. At dinner I get to meet two of my cousins, with whom I have had very little contact. Hundreds of children came out of the Kaye's Irish family of twelve, so it is no surprise that many of us do not know each other. And given that I left the US when I was twenty years old, there have been few opportunities to meet. I am deeply appreciating this moment.

Those years of pain are far behind. Very quickly, we begin to laugh with one another and appreciate each other as adults. One of the most heart-opening moments comes as my uncle helps me see something I have never been able to grasp. I never liked

Betty, my grandmother on my mother's side of the family. From my perspective, she was very critical and not particularly loving. My few memories of her were telling me things like, "You do not appreciate your mother. You are spoiled children with no sense of responsibility."

When it comes to thoughts or memories of Grandma, I have nothing positive to say. She was just a burden that rolled in once a year for a month, pointing out whatever did not suit her.

When Betty was in the house, my mom would change to accommodate her. There was always a sense of unease. Grandma would often sit in the same spot in the house reading romance novels. She always carried several in her suitcase. We'd have very few interactions, and the ones we did have centered mainly around the language I was using. I don't have a single memory of her hugging me.

Although it is not comfortable to say, I share, "I must tell you, I honestly never really loved Grandma. In fact, if I'm very honest, I really just felt like she didn't like me and I didn't like her." It is an honest sharing without any sense of vindictiveness. But I cannot anticipate how he might react.

He looks at me and smiles. In a soft-natured manner, he says, "Yeah, I can understand that."

I'm surprised because I expected him to defend his mother. I feel a great release. It has been on my mind and I am able to let the feeling be, without needing to explain or justify my feelings from childhood.

He goes on to give me a great gift. He tells me, "You need to understand what brought her to that point. When her husband was fifty-five years old, he went to the hospital for a routine biopsy, in which his gallbladder was accidentally cut. His body was being poisoned from within. The doctors went in one more time, which only compounded the original mistake. He died two weeks later. She was in her forties with twelve children.

"She spent the next twenty-five years alone. She survived that time by losing herself in romance novels. She did everything she could to rekindle the romance she lost when the one man she wanted to grow old with died suddenly."

It hits me that my grandmother, the woman whom I judged for so many years, and I were very much alike. Her life was very much determined by her husband's death, while mine has been determined by the death of my mother. It is the first time I've had the chance to understand and humanize my grandmother.

I knew of my grandfather's death, but as a young child, I never gave it any thought. It did not touch me directly, so it was a concept, a story. It dawns on me that there is so much in my life, especially childhood memories, where my perspective was only about my feelings and not those of others.

I ask, "How did you deal with her emotional shutdown?"

He says, "I am happy she found an outlet to connect to the pain of her loss. She navigated life the best way she could. When she would sit in the corner reading for hours on end, I would nudge her and say, 'You need to spend some time with the family.' Sometimes she would join and other times she wouldn't. In the end, it was her life."

To be able to see the real person behind that severe exterior is a beautiful moment that changes my feelings for her immediately. I have often noticed that not knowing the background of another makes it easy to judge. I have been given the gift of seeing my grandmother for the very first time.

After a wonderful day of visiting and reconnecting, it is time for our evening session. It is held in a shared communal space at the top of the same building where my aunt and uncle live. It looks like an old lounge from a nightclub where Frank Sinatra might have sung. All the furniture is dark wood and the chairs are upholstered in thick leather.

While setting up for the session, I see that my aunt has

underestimated the emotions that could arise during the session. I explain, "I need to move all of the tables away so that we can sit in a big circle. I don't want anything getting in between me and the participants. I have found that tables make it easier for people to hide."

She smiles uneasily, wondering what she is getting herself into. Over the next thirty minutes, their friends begin to arrive, about twenty people in total. Everyone sits in the circle and I share the same story that I have already shared in about thirty sessions so far. Each time I share it, I look in the eyes of participants and feel with them. The story is becoming less relevant than the emotional space we are sharing.

I am learning that I create the space not by sharing the story, but by allowing people to see the most wounded parts of myself. I use the word "space" often. In that word, I identify the size of the emotional space in which I allow people to join me. I envision a large circle. The more vulnerable I am, the more opportunity I give for people standing outside to join me.

If I am unable to allow my own vulnerability, the circle will be smaller and there will be more standing outside of it. The more I can allow my own vulnerability, the larger the space and the higher likelihood that people will not need to join. Rather they'll simply find themselves in it.

By creating space for vulnerability, we all heal each other. As the facilitator of the space, I feel like a "wounded healer," not here to teach or fix, but simply to connect to a sad part of my life. I have stopped using the filter of "appropriate" and "inappropriate." I can tap into the flow of universal feelings all humans share. And in allowing my emotions, they move through me and do not get stuck. I've noticed that the sessions themselves are not exhausting, but the trips between them are. If I hold back any emotions, I pay for it with exhaustion. When I don't hold back, the sessions are exhilarating.

After everyone writes their letters, I ask the group if they'd be willing to share, as I've done so many times. One man in the group is suffering from a very aggressive form of prostate cancer. He opens up and shares his challenges. He is undergoing hormone treatment, which compounds his feelings.

He shares, "I am very emotional now, and it feels terrible to place that burden on others. I have been struggling with this disease for over three years and the strain has been so great that I often find myself in tears. I feel like such a burden when I engage people in this state. I wish I wasn't so emotional."

I smile at him and say, "Yes, you could do that. But that isn't going to help anyone."

"Well, what would be the alternative?" he asks.

I share, "What if being emotional with others is actually part of the healing process for you? I have found that sharing my emotions allows people to connect with their own emotions. Instead of judging your emotions, I'd like to invite you to consider them a gift."

The idea is so contrary to what he has experienced that he stares at me blankly. It is at odds with all the judgment he has carried for so long.

I continue, "Most people are struggling to feel their emotions. If somebody in a group is able to allow them, and at the same time not judge them, they actually help others to feel. To be honest, not being emotional is really more of a problem for others than being emotional."

I am still speaking a foreign language to him, but he is listening attentively.

"The only reason I can be in this space at this moment is because I have allowed myself to be emotional. And you see what being emotional creates." The people in the group nod their heads in agreement. "Everyone here is grateful for your emotion and we appreciate that you are guiding us by taking the lead."

His eyes water as he gives himself permission to allow his feelings to surface. My aunt says, "I'd love to be closer to you and I would appreciate all of your emotions to come out. Nothing is too great."

I see him soften and I ask if he'll be willing to try an experiment. I say, "Could you say the following: 'I am overly emotional at inappropriate moments and it's fucking great.'"

He looks at me strangely as if to say, "Is this a joke?" But then he repeats the statement several times. Each time he becomes softer. Each time he relaxes into acceptance of himself. "'I am overly emotional at inappropriate moments, and it's fucking great. I am overly emotional at inappropriate moments, and it's fucking great."

He laughs. As do all those sharing the experience. He looks at me in the eyes and says, "Thank you. I needed that."

Many participants share their letters. It's time for me to share mine, which I have written to Death:

> *Dear Death,*
>
> *I have thought about you often, and then again, avoided thinking of you even more. You were scary and uncomfortable, yet you taught me more than you'll ever know.*
>
> *In your presence, I have learned the beauty of life and the preciousness of this limited time we have here. I have often said these last days that I was okay to meet you. That there has been nothing left unsaid. I'm grateful to you for guiding me and forcing me to focus on the essential and not get lost in the irrelevant.*
>
> *I do not want you to think that I'm looking forward to meeting you! I have many more years that I'd like to spend here. Yet when you do decide to visit, I will welcome you in, just like I have every other person in my life. With*

love and gratitude for giving me this time to share space with the others that are all waiting to greet you.

There are times when the thirteen-year-old self kicks in and I feel all my fears rise up. Then I realize that that thirteen-year-old never had the opportunity to hear you say that you love him. That you would take care of him. And that you'd be holding a space for him. I thank you for what you have given me, and I'm eternally grateful for every day you allow me to be of service on this earth.

I love you!

Andy

Although I have written this letter to Death, I decide to read another one which I wrote to my uncle a day earlier in Lincoln:

Dear Uncle John,

I'm sitting in Lincoln, Nebraska thinking of you. I write a letter at each session and, as I will be seeing you tomorrow, I wanted to use this moment to thank you. I know how important you were to Mom and I'm grateful you were so supportive to her as she went through life's challenges.

I appreciate the time and effort you have made to keep the family together. When I went to the last family gathering, I felt a deep appreciation for the love and caring I was shown.

I forgot that I was not only writing about my mother, but I was also writing about everyone else's sister. It is hard for me to imagine Mom's life before I came into it. Clearly, she also must have been a bit of a troublemaker to marry a Jewish man and end up in Los Angeles. In that way, I guess I am not all that dissimilar.

Thank you for being there. I know that taking care of my mother's arrangements with the craziness of my father and the conditions around the accident was more than I could comprehend at that moment.

With that I want to leave you with, I love you. These are the words that are often hardest for me to share, because in admitting my love, I also have to accept the possible loss. I no longer want to protect myself from that pain.

I love you!
Andy

After I finish, my uncle says with tears in his eyes, "I am looking around at all of these fathers in the room, and I'd like to say on our behalf that we are sorry that you had to go through that as a child. No child should have to experience that."

I feel the emotion of my childhood. The pain of not being seen. Even the pain of judging those who could not be there for me. And in the greatest irony, now that I am able to invite others to join me, I am given everything I was unable to receive as a child. Love and affection. I do not need to do everything myself. I can also be taken care of by others. Accepting this love is part of my journey.

As people leave this session, I feel compelled to hand my letter to Death to the man suffering from prostate cancer. I have no clear reason, but intuitively feel he might find it supportive. He thanks me and we give each other a hug and all leave for the night.

CHAPTER 27

Overcoming Perfection

(Des Moines, Iowa)

*I*t is my final night in Des Moines and I have the opportunity to spend it with one of my cousins. She is very similar to many of the entrepreneurs I have mentored throughout the years. It is a familiar archetype: a desire to achieve, while being held back by limiting beliefs. Of course, we all hold limiting beliefs. But in this case it is very specific. I call it "The Perfectionist" archetype.

The paradox in entrepreneurship is that successful entrepreneurs tend to get things wrong, but adapt quickly. Perfectionists have a hard time with this. Their need to get it "right" disproportionately outweighs their need to get it done. As a result, they often delay projects, so they fail before even starting.

My cousin wants to open a zero-waste business in Des

Moines. I see in her someone who needs to do it "right." She shares, "I have often felt that I have had something to prove. As the youngest in my family, there is a part of me that is very tied to establishing myself."

"What exactly is a zero-waste business?" I ask.

She says, "It means there will be no packaging and everyone will bring their own containers to transport from the store whatever they have purchased."

"When is it going to open?"

I see a look of dread wash over her face. I immediately recognize that she has been asked the question several times before and it touches something in her.

Before she can answer, I say, "My intentions to ask were purely out of curiosity. I certainly did not intend to put any more pressure on you." Her face softens. I am not sure she realizes how apparent her reaction actually was. I add, "You have nothing to defend or justify, I am just wondering when you thought it might open."

She answers, "Well, the plan was to open three months ago, but the contractors have not done as they promised."

I can see that any further questions about the opening date will push my cousin further into defense. I say, "It appears that this whole thing is weighing heavily on you."

She sighs. "I have not been able to get the contractors to finish their work and I'm very frustrated."

She is going through the frustration that just about anyone who has ever dealt with a building contractor experiences. It's always two times more expensive and takes two times longer than planned. But saying that is not going to help. Her expectation is clearly that it would have been done, so she sits in a perpetual state of tension. Asking when it will be completed is a reminder of what she has failed to achieve, namely, getting the store done at the original time she had set.

I do believe that just about anyone in the same position

would be frustrated. What I recognize as her greatest challenge is how to allow the frustration without succumbing to helplessness.

I ask, "How willing are you to accept that it is progressing slower than expected?"

She replies, "Not at all."

"Would you be willing to try something?" I ask. "How does it feel if you say, 'I am slow, incapable, and failing and it's fucking great?'"

"I can't say that," she protests. "I can say it could go better, but not that it's failing."

I laugh and say, "That's exactly the reason why I want you to say it that way. If you say, 'It has room to improve,' you are missing the point of the exercise. When you are completely comfortable with the thought, you no longer feel any defensiveness when the topic arises. You are free to act creatively. At the moment, most of your energy is going to anger and frustration. You're not creative when you're anxious. You're just fighting yourself. What if you could turn that energy into creativity?"

"That would be great," she says. "But if I accept that it's great, that means that I will be okay with what's going on."

I explain, "It isn't like that. Just because you find peace inside yourself does not mean you won't do anything about it. In fact, you are far more likely to do something about it. It just won't be reactive. It won't come from a place of defensiveness. You'll be open to considering new approaches to dealing with things because you won't be so self-critical."

She rationally understands, but still feels deep resistance.

I encourage, "Just give it a try and see how you feel. You can judge after you've given it a shot."

She smiles as if she is going to do something naughty. "I am incapable and it's fucking great. I am incapable and it's fucking great." She smiles as the release comes over her. She asks, "How does it work?"

I explain, "It's not that you're saying this to resolve your logical self. You say it to quiet the voice of your ten-year-old self. The one who isn't comfortable not being at the top of her class. The one who's not fully embracing that she doesn't need to be perfect to be loved. To be successful and so on."

Her boyfriend is sitting next to me and says, "It's exactly like when my brother was being bullied and someone said to him, 'You're a real asshole.' Instead of him fighting and defending it, he said, 'Yeah, I am an asshole, and what's it to you?' as he laughed."

I reply, "Yeah, exactly. He didn't allow that negative energy to come inside and define him. He embraced it and made it his own. So now he could be more fully integrated and emotionally capable of moving beyond it."

I leave both of them with a suggestion. I tell him that if he ever experiences his girlfriend being self-critical, to ask her if she'll be willing to embrace the thing she is judging and simply say, "It's fucking great."

As we sit together the rest of the night, there are three occasions when he observes something resembling self-judgment. As he points it out, my cousin replies, "It's fucking great." All of us laugh as she does it over and over again, making peace with the thoughts that just moments earlier were totally inappropriate.

It is a space of freedom that I am sharing with many people in my life now. A space where the emotions that were hidden in the shadows are drawn into the light, and loved.

CHAPTER 28

Finding Buddhism in Bloomington

(Bloomington, Indiana)

Frank is a professor at the Jacobs School of Music and a lay teacher in the Soto Zen tradition. He teaches courses on meditative practices and music.

I met Frank a few months earlier on the suggestion of a mutual friend. I gave him my original manuscript of *The Last Letter* in its messy form. He read it in one night and told me, "You kept me up last night. I couldn't put it down. It was a mirror of my own life. I too left the US with no money in my pocket to figure out what I really wanted."

I've arrived in Bloomington to see Frank. As I walk into his office, we greet each other like brothers, even though this is only the second time we've met. He tells me, "Whether you know it or not, you're a Zen Buddhist."

What draws us together is our mutual love of paradoxical relationships. Those things in life that appear contradictory, but in fact are complementary. The last time we met, we spent a lot of time discussing things like holding two opposing views in your consciousness simultaneously, and at the same time, not falling into one or the other as truth. For example, in order to free yourself of something that makes you defensive, you must first admit that you are that thing. Or, to support people, often the best thing you can do is not support them.

We walk across the campus to grab a coffee. As we sit on a bench looking onto the campus, he describes how he is using meditative practices in his classes. "The students are sitting with so much noise in their heads that a large part of my job is to help them see that there is an alternative way of experiencing the world."

I laugh and say, "I don't know if I have the patience anymore to spend the time to help people in that state."

He says, "If you're a fish in water, you don't know air exists. One of the practices I use is to show images that trigger emotional responses and immediately ask, 'Where do you feel it?'"

He explains he is often met with confusion when he asks this question. "What do you mean, 'where'? Don't you mean 'how'?"

Then he clarifies, "No, I mean where. Where in your body do you feel the emotion? Where is the sensation?"

He says it sometimes takes a while, but eventually the students begin to feel into their bodies. He says, "You see how quickly people shift, once they see that it is possible to experience themselves in an entirely different way. It's curious how people react to this. They will often have a different sense of how they experience themselves, and it is so foreign that they jump back into their heads. The need for logic hijacks the raw experience."

I reply, "Yes, I know this phenomenon well. Once a person feels the more sensual way of experiencing the world, if it's foreign, people tend to jump back into their brains and try to make sense of the experience. When I see this moment nowadays, I say, 'No, go back to where you were. That place before you tried to make sense of what you were seeing.'"

Frank replies, "Once they feel the sensation, I ask them to feel how it moves inside of them. I'll instruct them to feel into the tension, if it comes up. People are so unaware of tension that simply pointing it out creates a whole different awareness. I gently increase awareness around how people respond to it. Feeling the constriction is often the first step in allowing people to see into themselves."

We continue discussing the similarities in how we approach the world. We especially enjoy observing the confusion in the world of gurus who profess to be "beyond identity." I use the word identity here in place of the word ego, to highlight a state where people profess to have elevated themselves above the world of personal identification. Sometimes they will even go as far as claiming enlightenment.

We laugh out loud at the idea that for a person to claim that they are enlightened, they would need to project that onto themselves, thereby contradicting the statement. We are very much appreciating the utter absurdity of being in touch with anything other than everything that is, just as it is.

Frank shares, "I will see the thoughts arise and the emotions that arise from them. I will tend to nurture them until the feelings disappear again. At least on a good day."

We take this moment to connect back to our favorite topic: this interplay between the drastically different states of emotion and logic that are often in competition in our brains.

I say, "The interplay between the determined mind and the state that is just being one with everything is always shifting inside of me. The more I lean in either direction, the more I feel myself unaligned."

Frank responds, "I know that dynamic well. If I am out of balance, I feel it immediately. I see that people want to believe that this state of a quiet mind is something you reach, but that is far from the truth. There's not a constant state, but rather a fluctuating state that is often not evident to the individual."

It dawns on me that we are all sitting with this constant tension between wanting to get somewhere and wanting to feel at peace with everything just as it is. I realize I have tripped my way into Buddhism. We have come by different routes to the same apparent destination—both confused and at peace with that. Both laughing at the absurdity of life, without needing to solve anything. Just sharing an hour of time and loving one another.

CHAPTER 29
"I'm Not a Good Mother."

(Cincinnati, Ohio)

Jan is a man I've been mentoring for years. He founded several pharmaceutical companies throughout the Northeast and comes from a family of achievers. Two of his brothers are CEOs of their own companies. We've gone through many challenges over the years, and grown closer through it. In many ways, we have become family.

Jan has arranged for me to meet with three of his relatives, all of whom will be hosting sessions. One of these relatives is his Aunt Miriam.

I arrive at Miriam's house in Cincinnati, Ohio on a Sunday afternoon. The weather is miserable. Rain and wind whip in every direction. Miriam is a force of nature, too. She's seventy-eight, but her energy feels like a thirty-five-year-old.

I'm surprised when, after we greet, the first words out of her mouth are, "My son has put me in the penalty box for the last couple of years. He won't see me or allow me to contact him. I don't know how much longer he'll stay away from me."

I walk into the house and I am stunned by the incredible attention to detail. Everything, from the scent of the soap to the art on the walls, has been carefully selected and positioned to perfection.

She shares, "I am a recovering alcoholic and many of the people coming tonight are people from Alcoholics Anonymous."

Although I have never been to an AA meeting, I assume that the people coming have done a lot of emotional development work, as I see in Miriam. I wonder how it will be to share my story and how it may pale in comparison to what others have gone through. I then realize how absurd it is to compare anyone's story to another's, and this voice quiets in my head.

It's not long before Miriam comes back to the subject of her son. She says, "I have struggled throughout my entire life with our relationship. He's forty-nine years old, and age hasn't changed him much." She tells me she has made peace with it, but her reluctance to let it go shows that there is still pain.

I ask, "Is it okay if we interact a bit around the situation with your son?"

"Yes, of course," she says. "What do you see?"

I say softly, with the invitation to reflect, "I believe what I see is that you're still judging yourself for being a bad mother. In fact, it seems you don't believe that you are a good mother."

Immediately, tears start flowing. "Damn you," she says softly. "Yes. I have never felt that I could make up for the past."

She shares the details that make her feel this way. She summarizes by saying, "Regardless of what happens, my son blames me for everything he is unable to deal with in his own life."

I ask, "Are you open to trying an experiment? It's something that I have been playing with during my trip."

"Yes," she readily agrees.

I explain, "I have often found that when we repress an emotion in ourselves, it becomes a recurring thought, something that we struggle against. Instead of trying to manage that thought, as I imagine you've done with your son, I'd like to ask how it feels if you simply embrace it. How is it if you say, 'I was not a good mother, and it's fucking great.'?"

She has the same strange eyes I've become accustomed to. "No, I don't know if I could say that."

I say, "I know. But how about you give it a try? 'I was a terrible mother, and it's fucking great.'"

She takes a long moment and finally utters the words. "I was a terrible mother, and it's fucking great." It's not long before I see her relax as the epiphany hits.

As it sinks in, she utters, "Wow." After another long pause, she says, "If I try to manage the emotions, I am still a slave to them and they have power over me. The only way to let go of the emotions is to fully embrace that they are a part of me."

I smile. "Yeah. You're very quick with this one."

We spend the next hours laughing and appreciating one another. She makes a big pot of soup that is so delicious that I eat three bowls, even though I'm not hungry. I share that I have developed stomach acid because of all the horrible food I have been eating through the Midwest. She pulls out some special oils she uses to reduce the acidic content. I immediately feel better. She is doing everything she can to support me.

I am reminded of my time with Sharon and Darya and my challenge with receiving love and care. These incredibly giving people challenge my sense of independence. Pushing away love and support has been my control mechanism, a way to reduce the potential risk of losing control. I know this all too well since the death of my mother. But Miriam is so kind and thoughtful that I do not have much choice but to surrender to her giving.

Evening comes, and Miriam's friends begin arriving for the session. There are sofas positioned on three sides so I can sit in the middle. With the exception of one person, everyone present is a recovering alcoholic, or at least has had quite a lot of contact with alcoholism in their lives. It does not feel as if this is just another group. There is obviously a special bond among them.

I share my story as I have so many times before. Although this time, I pay close attention to the eyes of each participant. I think of all the times I have heard the phrase, "My name is _____ and I am an alcoholic." Now I am the one confessing my past. I see that these people have, to a large degree, made peace with the shadows of their past.

As the session comes to a close, there is a special moment when Angie, a friend of Miriam's, shares, "I'd like to take a moment to share my gratitude for Miriam and what she has meant to me."

I see Miriam look down, deflecting the praise. I know this very well because I suffer from the same constriction. I have begun to see this as another one of life's great paradoxes: the connection between pain and love. The fact that in order to fully experience love, we must fully be willing to embrace pain. By finally accepting the loss of my mother, I was able to embrace the love I had pushed away for so many years.

In this beautiful moment, when Miriam is receiving praise, she has learned to protect herself, too. Instead of allowing it in, she says, "I am grateful to all of you." She does anything to move away from the emotions Angie's praise has triggered.

I ask Angie, "Could you please say it again? Only this time, do not stop until you believe she has fully received it."

Angie gets up from her seat and kneels down in front of Miriam, holding both of her hands as she begins to speak. Miriam begins to giggle. I say, "Nope, you don't get to step away from this moment."

Angie says, "My life is so much richer because you are in it. You have been an example for me of hope and joy. You have taught me how to appreciate and love unconditionally."

As they see eye to eye, tears stream down Miriam's face. She embraces this beautiful moment without lessening it through humor or deflection. They both hug and the group follows to express their appreciation for Miriam and what she has meant to them through the years.

Everyone disappears until the two of us are alone again. I can see that Miriam has been pondering our previous discussion, and she's bursting with questions. She says, "I see that I move away from the intimacy, but it's a hard pattern to break. I do it to protect myself, and it's ingrained in me. I don't see people meeting me when I show vulnerability."

I laugh and say, "That's interesting. You acknowledge that you are protecting yourself by not fully showing yourself, but then you blame others for not being fully vulnerable. How does that work?"

She laughs as if her hand is caught in a cookie jar. "Yes, that's true. I am protecting myself through humor, through caretaking, and now, I see, through the avoidance of pain."

We speak until late in the evening. True to form, the next morning Miriam has a healthy breakfast waiting for me. Our conversation begins where we left off the night before. I ask, "How would your life be different if you allowed intimacy and embraced it?"

She says, "Completely, but I often feel unseen. As if people do not have the capacity to fully see me. How is it for you?"

"I don't expect people to see or understand me, so I guess I am not all that upset when they don't. I'd say, I am not dependent on people seeing or understanding me to feel at peace."

She smiles. "Well, that feels like freedom."

I say, "Yes, that certainly is freedom. And how would it be for you if you looked at those instances where you shut down emotionally in your life and decided to no longer hide, and give people the opportunity to truly see you?"

She says immediately, "Well, that's going to be most difficult with my family. I am fine with everyone else, but not my family. Once I'm with family, I don't feel the same. I start to fall back on my old techniques of survival. Telling jokes so that I can be characterized as the 'difficult one' in the family, the confrontational one with the big mouth."

I say, "What I hear you say is that you use that character of yourself to deal with the pain."

She nods. "Exactly. I have used these coping mechanisms to lessen the emotional separation I feel with my family."

"How would it look different if you were to show up and did not need anything from the family? What would you say? How would you interact differently?"

She says, "Well, I can see a glimpse of it. Instead of trying to alleviate the tension with humor, I can share it. I can share the emotions going on behind the frustration."

She continues, "It's a tricky moment because it's easy to turn it into halfway emotional. I see that telling someone how I am feeling is what I have done until now, and it doesn't work. It pushes them away. I need to share the vulnerability, and that is altogether different."

I reply, "Yes, I see that happen. People say, 'I am going to tell you my truth and now you have to deal with it.' They believe it is vulnerable, when in fact it is defensive. It's a common pattern that, as soon as we feel ourselves to be victimized, we in turn victimize others. We blame the other for how we are feeling."

Miriam identifies with the feeling of victimization and sees pushing others away as a pattern in her life. She asks, "What is an alternative?"

I answer, "It might look something like this: Instead of telling people what they are doing to you, you can share how it's affecting you. You can share the emotional impact without assigning blame. For example, 'I am feeling a lot of pain as I hear you speak.' As opposed to, 'You are making me feel uncomfortable.' In the former, you're not assigning blame. In the latter, you are forcing the other to take responsibility for your feelings."

After a short silence I ask, "What if you felt the pain and let that guide you?"

Her eyes immediately fill with tears and she says, "Well, then I would always be in contact with myself."

I reply, "Exactly. And how does that feel?"

She says, "Beautiful and scary. The world wouldn't define me anymore. I wouldn't censor myself to accommodate others. I would be comfortable regardless of where I found myself."

I say, "Exactly. So how does it feel to step into that world right now?"

She smiles, comes over and gives me a hug. "Thank you for coming into my life. You are a gem." We spend some more moments lingering in the feeling of appreciation for our connection before I need to get on the road to get to Pittsburgh, where I'll be visiting Jan.

CHAPTER 30

Success is Not a Destination

(Pittsburgh, Pennsylvania)

When I arrive in Pittsburgh, Jan tells me that the session he had arranged has been cancelled. The father of his wife, Amanda, has just undergone an operation to remove cancer from his chest. She is still recovering emotionally and doesn't want to add the stress of hosting a session.

As a single child, Amanda has been very close to her parents her whole life. The thought that she might lose one of them overwhelms her. She tells me, "As soon as I heard my father was diagnosed with cancer, I set aside a night to write everything I had to say to him." She shares what she told her father and what he means to her, everything he has done for her that has changed her life. She cries as she speaks of him.

She says, "I couldn't write it on paper because I needed to send it to him as soon as possible. I didn't feel like I had a minute to waste. I sent it as an email."

She tells me that her parents printed out the letter and framed it in their house. She tells me, "I'm grateful I was given the opportunity to share this. If I hadn't known you and we hadn't spoken about *The Last Letter*, I would not have done it."

Emotions are running wild in their house. I've never experienced the family this way. There is a gap in everyone's capacity to hold emotional space for each other. The pain in each family member is too great. Each is suffering in his or her own way.

It is hard not to jump in and make an effort to help. But I have learned that support is often most beautiful when it comes in the form of silence. Listening to each person as they process the pain that's looking to find a way out.

I spend four days with Jan and Amanda. It's time for me to head to my next destination, Boston. It's a ten-hour drive, and at the end of it, I will see my wife, Rani, who has flown from Amsterdam to Boston. We haven't seen each other in two months and we've both experienced a lot of change in this time. The day I left for my tour, Rani began a new job.

This is also a big day because an article I submitted to the website Buzzworthy has been published. My friend, the owner of Buzzworthy, very generously offered his support by publishing the article for exposure.

When people have asked about my aspirations for the journey, I say, "I am dropping kindling wood and setting little fires, not quite sure where it will all lead." But truth be told, I have built up the expectation that this will be a pivotal moment. I am hoping this article will go viral.

I found similar stories on the website that went viral. They were letters written by people soon before their death. The most recent one was by Holly Butcher, who died of cancer in 2018. She wrote a touching letter to the world, of which this is a portion:

> It's a strange thing to realize and accept your mortality at twenty-six years young. It's just one of those things you ignore. The days tick by and you just expect they will keep on coming; Until the unexpected happens. . . .
>
> That's the thing about life; It is fragile, precious and unpredictable and each day is a gift, not a given right. . . . I don't want to go. I love my life. I am happy. I owe that to my loved ones. But the control is out of my hands. . . .
>
> I just want people to stop worrying so much about the small, meaningless stresses in life and try to remember that we all have the same fate after it all so do what you can to make your time feel worthy and great, minus the bullshit. . . .
>
> You might have got caught in bad traffic today, or had a bad sleep because your beautiful babies kept you awake, or your hairdresser cut your hair too short. Your new fake nails might have got a chip, your boobs are too small, or you have cellulite on your arse and your belly is wobbling.
>
> Let all that shit go. I swear you will not be thinking of those things when it is your turn to go. It is all SO insignificant when you look at life as a whole. I'm watching my body waste away right before my eyes with nothing I can do about it, and all I wish for now is that I could have just one more birthday or Christmas with my family, or just one more day with my partner and dog. Just one more. . . .
>
> Tell your loved ones you love them every time you get the chance and love them with everything you have.

I see the impact of her message and I want people to live with the same sense of urgency that she had. I want to offer an example of how you can live if you accept that your life might be over tomorrow.

But as I have learned, big expectations don't tend to pan out. This expectation is no different. The link is emailed to me. The article itself is wonderful. It is very extensive and gives an overview of what I am doing and everything surrounding it. People find the article "nice" but it is not forwarded. It is not gaining momentum on its own.

Apparently, this journey cannot be about building something global. It needs to remain as it began—an opportunity to share intimate moments with others. I laugh and embrace that this is as far as I can bring it now. I have no intention of quitting, or judging it as anything less than a complete success. I just embrace with love and honesty that dedicating these three months of my life will need to be enough.

I am becoming aware of another of life's paradoxes. The more we strive to achieve, the more we forget that the real value of achievement is in the process, not the final accomplishment. Success is not a destination. It's a state of mind. I am beginning to feel success. I am not living on the sidelines of life and pointing at what is not possible. I am doing what feels to be impossible. I laugh at how quickly my brain is hijacking the beauty of the moment with ideas of what more can be achieved.

Now, on this ten-hour drive to pick up Rani, I reflect on the fact that I have done forty sessions in the past two months. When I decided to do this, I did not have a single session arranged, nor had I given a session. Two months later, I am thinking what more it can become. It's amazing how quickly we forget where we've come from and miss out on the beauty of the moment.

Dinner with my friend and mentor, Ray.
Balboa Island, California

The beautiful view of the mesas.
Sedona, Arizona

The attention seeking acts on Fremont Street.
Las Vegas, Nevada

My 3–month travel companion.
Santa Fe, New Mexico

The yellow brick road to Valley View Hot Springs
Villa Grove, Colorado

The dormitory at Valley View Hot Springs.
Villa Grove, Colorado

Meeting the local police.
Cleveland, Ohio

Message written on bench at Indiana University.
Bloomington, Indiana

I am glued to my navigation.
Albany, New York

Meeting Rani after 2 months away.
Cape Cod, Maine

My unreliable friend.
Manhattan, New York

167

The homelessness throughout the US is rampant.
Manhattan, New York

An emotional session.
Gaithersburg, Virginia

Ice storm at Thomas Jefferson's home.
Charlottesville, Virginia

My last session at the retirement community.
Miami, Florida

CHAPTER 31

The Limitations of Identity

(Albany, New York)

After a break in Allentown, Pennsylvania, I head to Albany, New York. On the way, I pick up Rory, the daughter of a dear friend.

When Rory was born, she was given the name Irene. But when she was about fifteen years old, she went through an identity crisis and changed her name. At that time, she wasn't quite sure if she wanted to identify as a male or female. This uncertainty lasted for about three years, then she finally ended up declaring herself lesbian. As she says, "I just got tired of needing to explain it to people."

When I pick her up, she's wearing hard-toed boots, short-cut hair, and a bold aviator jacket. The first thing she mentions is, "I am often misidentified as male."

We strike up an interesting conversation. She explains the evolving complexities concerning gender identity. It's no longer easy to be a lesbian because even lesbians are persecuted for their preferences.

What she goes on to explain is so complicated that I feel as if I need to write it down to fully understand it. She tells me that within the LGBTQ movement, gender identity, i.e. male or female, is different from sexual preference. Neither should be taken for granted or assumed. One may be a male, who identifies as a female and finds females attractive, or vice versa.

As Rory explains all of the variations, my mind begins to fold. It begins to feel more like an algebraic equation than a true understanding of human sexuality.

As I struggle to make sense of all the different combinations of gender identity and sexual preference, she throws a curveball at me. She says, "If a male identifies as a female and has the sexual presence of a woman, then the lesbian community is, in many cases, pressured to have sex with these individuals." The term used to describe it is the "cotton ceiling." Similar to women who have struggled to break through the "glass ceiling," those who identify as female, and have penises, are having trouble finding lesbian sexual partners. I am amazed at how far we have come in terms of identity.

To make it more explicit, she shares, "If a lesbian does not want to have sex with a person who gender identifies as female, regardless if they have a penis, then they are often labelled bigots."

The idea that someone would be expected to have sex with somebody they would not desire flies in the face of common sense. According to her, this has become such a big deal that she can't even talk about it publicly for fear of retribution.

I am utterly confused. I'm doing my best to support people to see beyond identity. In the realm of sexuality, identity has become critical to our sense of being. It is created and developed, encouraged and supported.

I've often seen that people identify themselves as "something" and by doing so, separate themselves away from broader society. A part of this is simply human. In our stages of development, at some point we are no longer at peace with just "being" and we distinguish ourselves from what is outside of us.

What I have seen in this process of identity-shaping is that the initial move to identity is most often a reaction to loneliness and fear. Once a person has adopted an identity, they often derive a sense of power from it. Sharing an identity strengthens us through a common purpose or a common enemy. Whether in politics, religion, or gender identity, once we have either nominated ourselves or been placed in an identity by others, we are usually blind to how that identity shapes us.

My thought has been that when we are stuck in any form of identity, we do not truly want to change anything. We only want to strengthen that identity. And an identity is strengthened by feeling more and more alienated. "You'll never understand."

As I travel through the US, I see this alienation on a scale that I could never have imagined in the realm of politics. Each side accusing the other of being "stupid," without realizing that the statement in itself stops any process of understanding each other. What I find most interesting, and so subtle that it may go unseen, is that the identity is not primarily about Republicans and Democrats. It is deeper. It is the idea that there is something "right." There is something "better." Something that the other one does not see. There is a subtle arrogance that no one tends to reflect on because they are "right."

Einstein said that a problem cannot be solved in the context in which it was created. To solve the challenges created by identity, we must move beyond identity. This is, of course, tricky. How do we move beyond something we are not aware of? How do we see what we do not see?

In my experience, this is a process of lessening the grip that our identity has upon us. Not allowing it to define us as much. To begin such a journey, we must first accept that we judge. We observe things and we place values on them. We do not need to stop it, but simply become aware that it is happening. Once that process is recognized, we have the chance to reprogram it in our system.

We arrive at the Catholic Youth Center where Rory works. We hold a session with her friends. This topic is a bit heavy for them, given their ages and their limited experiences with loss. Regardless, they ask me many questions regarding my journey and how I navigated the pain from the past.

I leave Rory and continue on my journey.

CHAPTER 32

Reuniting with Rani

(Cape Cod, Massachusetts)

*A*fter dropping Rory off, I drive to the Boston airport, where Rani has arrived from Amsterdam. I wait for her by the luggage belts. Finally, she appears. After two months apart, I'm thrilled to see her bright smile.

We hug one another tightly. After so much time away, we both feel a sense of wonder. Are you the same person I remember? What has changed? We look into one another's eyes for any trace of anxiety or fear. We are both quite sensitive and are not afraid to ask. We melt back into one another. She points out that I have a cold sore on my lip, which is always an indication that I am worn out.

Unfortunately, we have little time to speak because I have

a session at Brown University in less than two hours. I can see from Google Maps that we are running a few minutes late, even without traffic. We hit traffic, which adds stress to the drive. And as luck would have it, we can't find a parking spot. We drive around a few times until we finally find a space a few hundred meters away from the venue.

Rani is tired and tells me she will wait outside. She has not been to a session yet and has avoided such events in the past. She has never been particularly interested in my personal development activities, nor do I pressure her to join. She is continually supportive, so I cannot ask for anything more of her.

Six people show up, all young students. Since they have not experienced much loss in their lives, their interests lie more in my overall motivation for the trip. Each group I've been with creates a particular state that defines how the session goes. I liken it to a picnic. The session is only as good as the company and food everyone brings. In this case, there is not a lot to eat or talk about.

The session ends and I walk out to find Rani. It's now dark and we have a drive back to Boston, where we've booked a hotel. After two months without each other, we have two days together.

Unfortunately, the first thing on Rani's mind is not connecting, but administration. There are many things that have come up in the last weeks and she wants to use our time together to resolve all open administrative issues. It creates immediate tension. The better part of our first day together is strained around discussions on how to manage our housing situation. We've been told we have to leave the place where we've been staying for the last couple of years, and it has created deep anxiety in Rani.

We don't have any plans, and sense that connecting in the city won't be easy. I do a quick search to see places to visit nearby. I ask Rani if she's open to taking a short trip away. She's excited and says, "Yes." I notice the name Cape Cod. I know little about it, except that it's a vacation destination. I book a hotel and we leave.

Cape Cod is about an hour-and-a-half south. It's now fall in Massachusetts and the trees are glowing with colors. The ground, scattered with fallen leaves, looks like it's on fire. I feel like I am walking through an impressionist painting.

As we drive, we talk about where we are in our lives. It's clear something has changed. Rani asks, "What if we continue this way? We have both gone our own way these past months. What if this just continued? Where would we end up?"

I feel a mix of fear and curiosity. We have taken on our own projects at the same time, and neither of them appears to be bringing us together. I say, "I know I can't stay on the road for much longer, so at least we have a deadline." But I see her point. I did not anticipate how much this project would consume me. Although we have spoken each day, it has been between drives, meals, and sessions. Finding the time to simply connect has been challenging. I am beginning to wonder how my desire to do something with my life has gotten in the way of our relationship.

I am also feeling even deeper questions emerge. Before going on this trip, I was told many times that I was not living up to my full potential. That I was moving away from the talent I had been given and all the skills I had developed. I had let those voices build inside my head, which accumulated in a deep desire to do something.

That led to a rather abrupt decision to write a book and then take a journey. I am not exactly sure where it will lead me, or even why I am doing it. It is a calling. In retrospect, I am asking myself if it is just a means of me avoiding the pain of this life being meaningless.

I look at Rani and see I have the potential to lose the person I love most if I continue down this road. A road I thought would bring me closer to her is actually taking me further away. I laugh at the irony that I am creating space for hundreds of people, except the person who means the most to me. Through the years, we have always found our way back to one another. But I see that our current paths could move us so far apart that it will be hard to find ourselves together again.

We make it to our hotel. It is more like a motel, with the typical drive to your door. It is our second-to-last night together. Although it is cold, we decide to sit outside by the fire. About ten of the guests from the hotel are all bundled up in blankets around the fire. We're asked what we're doing here. We spend the next minutes discussing the contents of the book and the purpose for the trip. One woman across from me has tears in her eyes as she considers her last letter. I can see Rani next to me beaming with pride, as if saying, "I am married to this man" with her eyes.

The following morning, we make our way back to Boston where I have a session planned. It is our last night together, but the session was arranged long before Rani planned the trip. I tell her, "I am tired. Another month feels like an eternity."

CHAPTER 33

A Judgmental, Heartless Asshole

(Boston, Massachusetts)

*A*fter the rejuvenating getaway with Rani, I don't want to attend my next session. But I am committed to pushing through and accepting all emotions and circumstances.

I start the session by saying, "This is the first session I have not looked forward to." I don't know how my words will land. I just allow my present state to guide me.

I follow by sharing what I've gone through to get here and how hard it is to think that I still have a month left. No one takes offense. If anything, they appear to appreciate my candidness. In my experience, sharing my current state does not push people away, but rather gives them trust. If I am willing to show how I am feeling, regardless of whatever else I have to say, at least I am vulnerable.

The session appears to be like many of the others. There is a group of about eight, and many of them are meeting for the first time. I've learned that it does not really matter whether people know each other prior to the event. In some cases, groups are more intimate when participants don't already know each other.

What appears to be a better indicator of the emotional depth of the session is people's ability to hold space for one another. By holding space, I mean not jumping over emotions, and not using things like humor or diversion tactics to guide people away from their own discomfort.

One of my requests each session is that no one tries to heal anyone else. "We are here to witness, not to heal each other," I often say. Sometimes, these instructions are respected. Other times, the tension is too great and one or more of the participants falls into healing mode. I do not police this, as I accept that each session will become whatever it is meant to be. I am not trying to push for an outcome. I am surrendering to each moment, and the sessions take on their own unique flavors.

I see three factors that influence people's ability to "hold space." One is their age. I've often seen that the older someone is, the more he or she is able to accept things as they are. The second factor is life experience. People who have experienced trauma, regardless of age, seem to more easily see that there is nothing to solve. And finally, it is a measure of how much personal development work someone has done, how far they are able to see through their own emotional reactions.

When a group can hold more space for one another, magical things will often occur. This is one of those groups. As I begin the session differently, by sharing what I've been through, I share how radical self-love is a major theme that has emerged. I describe the tool I've been utilizing during the trip: taking the thing you judge most and loving it, completely and without reserve. I show how the reclamation process works. I notice many of the participants perk up as they ponder how it might affect their current struggles.

After a beautiful, open discussion, I give participants their instructions to write a letter. It turns out to be one of the longest letter-writing sessions, an hour. Although I always give the instruction that we'll spend about a half hour, if people are deep into their writing, I never disturb them.

When we come back and sit in a circle, a man stands and asks if he can share. He is so enthusiastic that there is no stopping him. He goes on to say, "I am fascinated by this discussion around radical self-love. I took it to heart and wrote a letter to my mother."

The group's curiosity is sparked and he is asked if he'll be willing to read it. As he reads through the long list of things that he now loves about his mother, we all laugh. It's clear that he no longer feels judgment towards these things he has judged and resisted all his life. He is free to laugh at all the things he took so seriously only a few minutes earlier. He appears to be a different person altogether. His posture changes. There is a sparkle in his eyes. He is shocked that something that weighed so heavily upon him for so many years could be lifted so easily.

Another man in the group uses the moment to share something that is also not easy. He says, "I am full of judgment. I had judgment towards you as you read your letter. I had judgment toward the people in the group who had tears in their eyes. I even had judgment of myself for not writing a more intimate letter."

The group bursts out in laughter. It is clear that he is enjoying the fact that he does not need to hide. He adds, "In all seriousness, I have a question about judgment. How do you not have it?"

I laugh and counter the question. "That's strange. How is it possible to live life without judgment?"

I recognize a challenge I've had to overcome myself. I had a judgment towards judgment. What my mentor helped me see was that in judging judgment, I created a problem for myself. As he said, you need to distinguish between judgment that is more or less personal in nature. I use this insight to help the participant.

"You've created a dilemma for yourself," I say. "You cannot avoid judgment. It's part of life. What you can do is heighten your consciousness around your judgments so that they no longer define you as much."

He looks curiously at me. "So you're telling me it's good to judge?"

I reply, "No, not exactly. Judging happens. It's part of who we are. We have our senses and they take in inputs. Our brains assimilate that information and create mental constructs so we can better understand what is going on around us.

"The challenge is seeing how much we project value onto our experiences. Are we viewing it, or are we placing a value on it? I use the term 'value judgment' as opposed to just judgment, because it is in valuing it—viewing it as 'good' or 'bad'—that we make it personal. Judgment is neither good nor bad. It's a necessity. Placing a value upon judgment is where we make it personal. And it is in this world of personal that problems often emerge. Especially when the values are blind to us."

He is getting clearer, but the thought is so much bigger than his current construct that he asks me to slow down.

I further explain, "We can't survive in the world without judgment, so just take it for granted. Our mind places value judgments on everything we see and experience. At that moment, we have a choice. We accept the value judgment without reflection, or ask ourselves, *What is it that makes me judge this?* In that answer, there is a wealth to discover, both about people you judge, and even more importantly, yourself."

He is still struggling to distinguish between what would make a judgment more or less personal. He asks directly, "How do I know if it's a value judgment? Or if I am making it personal?"

I say, "You know because of how you experience it when you say it. You are either entertaining the thought or you are convinced of it. When you said, 'The sniffling is annoying,' you stated it globally. As if you had some command on what is and is not annoying. By saying, 'Apparently, I have a problem with sniffling people,' you make it less personal by seeing that this is true for you, but not necessarily a universal, objective 'truth.'"

It's another one of those interesting paradoxes. In order for us to make things less personal, we need to make them personal to ourselves. We need to claim it, without stating it universally. "I find sniffling people irritating," or "I get triggered around sniffling people," is very different from, "Sniffling people are so irritating."

He remains curious. Every answer generates three more questions. He asks, "This has and continues to be a problem for me. What can I do about it?"

I reply, "Let's assume for the moment that you're triggered. There is something in your environment you're reacting to. The question is, how do you process it? At this moment, you can heighten your awareness and shift how you experience the world. Or you do what you've done until now."

"Please be more concrete," he says.

I reply, "Okay, the moment you recognize judgment, you'll feel emotions arise as you place a value on what you're seeing. At that moment, pause and embrace the feeling. If you don't, you'll struggle against it. In your case you'd say, 'I hate sniffling people, and it's fucking great.'"

He repeats it a few times and feels into himself. The room turns more serious.

"Once you've put your judgment to rest," I continue, "you can ask, 'What is it about people sniffling that is a problem for me?'"

His face immediately softens. His eyes water and it touches him. Here he sees through himself. He does not share what he sees, but we all recognize it is powerful. He shares his gratitude to the group for the extra time and ends by proclaiming, "I am a judgmental, heartless asshole, and it's fucking great."

There are more laughs as the group loses any need to impress one another. It is an intimacy that I could not have planned or imagined ahead of time. And it began with me saying, "This is the first session I have not looked forward to."

CHAPTER 34

Living with a Narcissist

(Boston, Massachusetts)

I met Ingrid about nine months earlier at a session in Northern California. She is hosting my final session in Boston at her home. When I arrive, she introduces me to her husband, Jim. I immediately sense tension in the air.

I am strongly empathic, so it's virtually impossible for me not to feel emotions from others. When I walk into a situation where a person is in tension, I can feel that same tension in myself. It used to overwhelm me. But once I learned how not to react to it, that became a skill.

At that same time, it became a threat to people who do not want to be seen. People want to believe that their emotions are invisible. But it's simply not true. We show ourselves in ways we can't even see. How we stand. How we speak. What we speak about. How we listen to others.

So I sit with Ingrid and Jim and ask, "How are things going?"

They quickly open up. Both share the troubles they are having with their mothers. They each tell me story after story revealing how absurd and horrible their mothers are. They both agree that their mothers are diagnosable narcissists.

More tension has been added to the situation because Ingrid has told Jim she won't allow Jim's mom to visit for Thanksgiving. Jim is being put in a tough position. By saying no, he will certainly encounter the wrath of his mother. I can almost see him cower in the chair as he imagines how that conversation will go.

I ask, "What would stop you from setting clear boundaries?"

As soon as the words leave my mouth, I feel anxiety arise in Jim. He replies, "My mom has been rejected by so many people in her life. I am the only one left. If I cut her off, she will have no one."

They share a recent moment when Jim's mother was shouting at him and Ingrid yelled back, "I won't let you speak to my husband this way." By inserting herself into the mix, Ingrid exacerbated the problem. Jim's mother stormed out of the room and the relationship has been on ice ever since.

After the incident, Ingrid realized she cannot protect her husband. It isn't her responsibility to manage his relationship with his mother. Nor can she truly separate her frustration with her own mother from that with Jim's mom. She can only take responsibility for herself. In order to do that, she has told Jim she does not want his mother coming to visit unless certain conditions are met.

Instead of Jim only needing to deal with his mother, he is now confronted with balancing the relationship between his wife and his mother. Jim longs for a relationship with his mother, although it brings him no joy. The pressure for him to be there for his mother is so great that he is having trouble imagining any scenario where Ingrid and his mother will both be satisfied. It is not working for anyone.

Jim is very much dependent on his mom. Although he says he wants to deal with it, he is a slave to an idea in his head. Namely, that he is the only person left who can help her, which is why he can't give up on her. As he puts it, "I have been taking care of my mom my entire life. I don't even know who I am if I am not doing that." His entire self-identity is connected to being a "good son." The crux of the problem is that he allows his mother to be the judge of what that actually means.

It is clear to me that if something does not shift, divorce is likely. Jim is not fully processing that, as he is still trying to control everything, including his wife. I can see this process is hard for him. He is in a prolonged, deep well of pain, and me stirring up the muck at the bottom is very threatening. But I want to see if I might be able to offer a glimpse of an alternate reality.

I ask, as I have so many times before, "Would you be open to an experiment?"

"Yes," he agrees.

I ask, "What would life look like if you could see the lightness in it all? What if you could laugh at how dysfunctional the situation has become? What if you simply said, 'I am incapable of dealing with my narcissistic mother and it's fucking great.'"

He plays along, but I see he lacks any desire to shift anything. People often change as a natural consequence of two things: either extreme pain that becomes unacceptable, or an inspiring vision of how life can be different. In his case, neither of these states exist. It appears he can sustain a great deal of pain.

I do not push any further. I see that I am heaping more and more on a person who is not ready to take the risks required to redefine his life. He has been walking on eggshells for years and anything that might shift that is too much. He cannot see that his entire life is defined by this fear. All of his relationships are being impacted because to protect himself, he shuts down emotionally.

Our time together runs out and it's time for the session. Jim decides not to participate in the session, which I find sad but not surprising. His emotions are raw and he does not want to be confronted with them in the group.

After the session is over, Ingrid receives a text from Jim. He tells her he will not be coming home until I leave. He found our interaction very uncomfortable and far too direct for his liking. He says he didn't feel safe. He did not get the emotional space he needed.

Both Ingrid and I are surprised, as we felt our time together was deeply connected, and it helped her address issues that had been building for years. She was getting exactly what she needed to build confidence in the relationship. But it was all too much for Jim.

I feel a mix of emotions. It is not the first time on this trip that I've seen someone react to my openness. As if another person is responsible for one's own emotional wellbeing. Many people struggle to engage in an open and frank way. They will use that struggle often as an excuse to project and blame. Instead of owning their emotions, "I feel uncomfortable with this exchange," they say things like, "You are too aggressive," or "You don't care how people feel."

The irony never ceases to amaze me. Once we blame someone else for our incapacity, we exhibit the same behavior that we are accusing him or her of. Namely, by accusing someone that he is too aggressive, we are passing judgment upon them, which is an aggressive act. This hardly goes noticed by the individual making the judgment. As they are the self-proclaimed victim, they therefore must defend themselves.

Just as I experienced with the neuroscientist in Esalen, being fully present emotionally isn't easy for someone incapable of allowing that in themselves. As I have seen, it's often rejected and blamed.

At this point in my life, my intention is to spend time with people in love. I have nothing to sell, nor do I require anything emotional in return. I am loving myself and others, without expectation. I am coming to grips with a new reality. If I choose to be "me" in whatever shape and form that takes, there will always be a percentage of people who cannot embrace "me," at least not in that manifestation.

I am beginning to see more clearly that self-sacrificing makes it all about the other's needs. Adopting self-acceptance makes it also about my own. I am no longer excluded. So being me will mean others may suffer. Not because of any desire from me to hurt them, but rather out of their own inability to embrace the parts they judge in me, which are in fact the parts they judge in themselves.

I have also learned that it's not enough to ask people if they feel uncomfortable with a discussion. Several times throughout my journey, I have seen people get uncomfortable. In every case, I have asked them if they are comfortable continuing. They almost always say "yes," but only because they have trouble saying "no." Instead of recognizing their inability to set boundaries, they blame the other for not seeing behind their "yes."

Although they permit the discussion, they feel resentment afterwards, a feeling as if they have been violated. They must be very protective of who they let into their lives. They only feel comfortable around people with whom they feel a sense of control. Because they can't take control of themselves, they need to manage everyone around them.

In the past, I would have given these people a lot of my time. There was a part of me that wanted to be seen. A part that felt bad for being judged. Now, at this point in my life, I don't get lost in others' incapacities. I can just love them. Even for their judgment. Especially because of their judgment. I know how hard it is to bear that burden. I have just chosen to let it be. It has made my life so much freer and easier.

In this case, I embrace that I will love in the way I know how. When Jim gets angry at me, I feel sadness and compassion. I do not blame him, nor myself. He is allowed to be who he is, and I am, too.

What I know is that I am not out to hurt anybody. It does hurt when I hear that someone was made to feel uncomfortable. But it's not taking priority. I am not self-editing in order to sidestep this potential pain when it arises. I am not the world's therapist. I am not trying to solve the world's problems, or even those of an individual in front of me. I have learned from years of experience that there is nothing more therapeutic than simply loving the thing you judge most.

I am a self-absorbed narcissist who has no feelings for anyone else, and it's fucking great. I step all over the feelings of others with complete disregard, and it's fucking great. I am aggressive and inconsiderate, and it's fucking great.

Instead of defending that I am not all these things, I embrace it all. And it's fucking great.

CHAPTER 35
Exploring Emotional Triggers
(Rhinebeck, New York)

The next morning, Rani and I get up and I drive her to the airport. It is not easy to say goodbye. It feels like just yesterday that she arrived and now I am dropping her back off. We are both feeling the weight of our changing lives and becoming increasingly aware of how we rely on one another for support. It is a beautiful goodbye. I watch her walk away. As she disappears, reality sets back in.

I begin the third leg of my journey, south down the East Coast. The next stop is Rhinebeck, New York, where I'm meeting Michelle, whom I met at a training I gave.

Michelle read the manuscript of *The Laster Letter* early on, well before it was published. It touched her so much that she sent it to her brother, who then sent it on to his friends. It was the first time I believed that this project may be greater than I was allowing myself to dream.

We also became close because her mother died not long after she had read the book. Both she and her brother wrote letters to their mother, which they read to her on her deathbed. They both shared the letters with me.

Michelle's mother is American and her father is English. She grew up with the cultural restraint of a proper Brit. Yet she is also very open to learning and growth. We hit it off quickly, because although my irreverent manner could be a bit shocking to her, she would never get offended. In fact, she enjoyed learning from the process.

The first time we met, I would deliberately make statements I knew would trigger her. I would watch her get triggered, but then immediately she would get curious to understand what was happening inside her. It became a bit of a game to intentionally create tension inside her to give her opportunities to learn about herself. She actually enjoyed it and wanted more of it.

When I arrive, I am welcomed with a surprise. Michelle is five months pregnant. She smiles and says, "I guess I should have told you."

She's eager to pick up where we left off in exploring her deepest emotional triggers. I say, "By the time I leave, I am going to help you see and move past those auto-responses. All the triggers that set you off."

She is up for the challenge and replies, "Yes, please! I have really wanted to work on this."

When she says the name of someone she likes, I say "She's such a bitch." I watch her body contract. Her mouth begins moving without connecting to the feelings that come up inside of her. Before letting her continue, I ask, "What's going on?"

She stops and reflects. She says, "I felt like I needed to defend her."

"What would your life look like if you didn't need to defend?" I offer. She smiles and encourages me to do it again.

We play the game for the next few hours. I trigger her. We stop and reflect. Then we discover something new. Each trigger is a window to another part of herself that she is seeing with more clarity than ever. Through the exercise, she is becoming more and more open. It is apparent how quickly a trigger occurs and that she is unaware when it is happening. There is no separation between the trigger and her response.

By practicing, she has the opportunity to feel the moment over and over again. In doing so, it is no longer an automatic response. There is more space to see what she is not seeing. She is trying to solve the emotion after it has been triggered, instead of seeing it the moment it occurs. In the latter case, life gets much easier because instead of managing our emotions, we are seeing them emerge. The more able we are to see them emerge, the freer we are to play with them, the freer we are to let them be without allowing them to define us. In essence, they no longer define us. Rather, they guide us.

What is becoming more and more apparent is that she is triggered by authority, and especially by men with strong voices. I put on my strong, authoritative voice in response to something she says and say, "That's nonsense."

She's triggered. She pauses and reflects. Then, her eyes widen and she says, "Give me a moment. I am beginning to see something here. My father was incredibly loving, but he was also very strong-minded. I see that there is part of that strong-mindedness that I have never come to fully accept. I have never been able to fully love."

I smile and ask, "Can you see how the inability to love and accept that part of you is also what's stopping you from loving your father?"

She nods. "Psychologically I understand that, yet it's still hard for me to embrace that in myself. There is an aspect in it that I don't want to become."

"And what is that?"

"I don't want to lose sight that there is always another point. There is always another thing to say that is being neglected or dismissed."

"Yes, that's always true. But what happens to you when you don't have the ability to carry the weight of that voice? Not that you need to, but what happens when you can't?"

She says, "People don't necessarily know where they stand with me. By my keeping things at a surface level and speaking in general terms, I ensure that people can't really get hold of me. It's a way to protect myself. I see how this is all showing up in my life. I just moved in with my husband and we are planning to have this child together. My husband is also quite strong-minded and I struggle to communicate important things to him because I worry that I won't be heard."

I laugh and say, "You married your father."

"Apparently," she laughs in return.

Her big realization comes when she says, "I see that when I get triggered, I can either step toward or away from myself. When I blindly react to a trigger, I am stepping away from myself. When I create space to explore my feelings, I am stepping towards myself."

We continue playing with the triggers as she slowly observes the process in herself. It's as if she has a magnifying glass pointing inward at the dark spaces she's never seen before. I have seen that it is exactly in these blind triggers that we lose ourselves. To the degree that these areas go unseen, they define us and our interactions with others.

A friend once shared a book of ancient wisdom with me. In it, the teacher spends the entire first year triggering the students, incessantly teasing them over and over again in order to heighten their triggers. Of course, the students don't know it is being done intentionally. It is each student's journey to realize that she is being defined by the world around her. Once the student sees the triggers, she can move them in new directions. Until that point, she is only a reaction to the trigger.

CHAPTER 36

Longing for Connection

(Rhinebeck, New York)

*A*fter exploring her triggers, Michelle has a request. She wants me to work with her and her husband, Josh, to work through issues they are having.

I say, "I am always happy to sit as a third party. But when it comes to couples, I have often seen that each partner wants to use the facilitator to justify his or her position to the other. When I make a point that supports one person, they will say something like, 'I told you so.' I can help, but I'd need both of you to feel comfortable acknowledging that you've been the problem all this time. I am not here to convince the other for you."

She agrees, as does Josh.

Josh has an eight-year-old son from a prior marriage.

Michelle is trying to figure out how not to feel like a third wheel when the three of them are together. She is longing for connection but having trouble because the boy is not hers and she doesn't feel comfortable imposing her wishes upon Josh. Namely, she wants to experience their time together as a family. Instead, she feels the three of them are living separate lives. Josh is with his child, while Michelle waits for him to return to her.

She has a hard time articulating what she is missing and Josh feels helpless. He clearly wants her to feel comfortable. He just doesn't know how to make that happen. She wants time for the family to bond, yet Josh doesn't know how to create that and Michelle doesn't know how to ask for it. At least not in a way that Josh understands what needs to change for her to feel the connection she is longing for.

She also shares her fear. "When our baby is born, I don't want your son to feel less loved."

One thing becomes clear quickly: They are having trouble not being triggered by the words of one another. When Michelle says, "I feel like there is a triangular relationship when your son is with us," Josh hears criticism instead of helplessness. As many men do, Josh tries to solve the situation, instead of just listening.

"How do I triangulate?" he says defensively. "I have tried hard to bring you in."

Michelle throws her arms in the air and looks at me. "This is how these conversations go. We always end up here. It always breaks down."

Before allowing the situation to escalate any further, I interrupt and ask, "How does this way of communicating work for you?"

Both acknowledge that it is not working, nor is it sustainable. I then proceed to ask, "How would it be if we took an entirely different approach?"

They both agree.

I am breaking a pattern I often see between people. People are triggered by one another and react without knowing what, in fact, they are reacting to. What is the emotion that is being triggered?

In the end, each wants to be seen. Michelle wants to be seen in her desire to create connection. Josh wants to be seen for being willing to find a way to make it work, and more importantly, for already making an effort. They each long for connection, but they can't find connection through their triggers. Since they cannot open up in vulnerability, they react over and over to unspoken pain.

I say, "Quite honestly, I am not really interested in what you are talking about. I'd rather discuss the way you go about discussing. I can help you solve this issue. But if we don't solve your approach to interacting with one another, there will be situation after situation and I won't always be here to help."

Both agree. I continue, "Michelle, when you tell Josh that he is triangulating you, he hears it as a judgment. You desire connection, but you are pushing him away with your statement. You're not embracing your suffering. You're stepping over it and blaming Josh for how you feel. Instead, how would it be if you let him see you and your suffering?"

Michelle then goes on to share her pain. It is not easy for her. Her "British restraint" makes it challenging for her to reveal the depth of the pain. But she tries. After a few sentences, the pattern kicks in as Josh feels that he is being blamed.

I allow him to speak for a moment and then point out the pattern. "You see how it works. You get triggered by something that has nothing to do with you, and both of you reinforce it in one another. For this moment, allow the other to speak, knowing you are not responsible for what they are feeling. They are their feelings. They are entitled to them. It does not make them true."

Michelle asks for guidance. "Can you help us here? Again, can you be more directive?"

I reply, "When you share with Josh, instead of thinking about him, could you please tell me what it feels like for you when they go off and play, leaving you alone? What are you longing for?"

She replies, "I am longing for connection. I am longing to feel we are a family unit."

I can see Josh fighting back the need to react. He can see in my eyes that I want him to hold back.

I ask, "Can you tell Josh what it feels like when it isn't a family?"

She is quiet and then begins to cry and she shares, "I am utterly anxious for when the new baby comes. I don't want for him to feel unloved."

Josh is exploding to respond and I ask him to just hold space for Michelle without needing to respond. I explain, "You don't need to solve this. You don't even need to respond. Just being with her in this anxiety is enough for the moment."

Josh is seeing that even though it goes against his natural impulse, Michelle is simply appreciating being fully heard, without needing to defend or justify herself.

We agree that there is no need to solve anything for the moment. Just giving it space will be enough to deal with it when it arises in the future. I say, "Hold it softly and you'll see that it will evolve. Try to solve it too soon and you'll notice that whatever you agree to at this moment will become stressful in the future."

Now that Michelle is on a roll, she wants to touch an issue that arises on quite a few occasions: money. It is an issue that is coming up with many of the families that I visit on this trip.

Josh and Michelle come from very different financial backgrounds. Josh's parents own a food truck and he sees his parents working hard, waking up early in the morning to run out the door and prepare food. His father really wants him to become part of that business. Josh decided early on to get an education in order to find a different way of life. He became a somatic therapist and built a practice in New Jersey near his ex-wife and son.

Michelle, on the other hand, comes from a wealthy family. Her father started and sold large pharmaceutical companies. They are just starting to build a life together with a child on the way. It is clear to me that there will be potential challenges in dealing with the financial integration of these two different worlds.

I ask, "How has it been working up until now?"

I can see from the response, or rather lack of a response, that it is an area that has no clear vision. I also sense a tension because they don't really know how to address it going forward.

I've seen money become an issue in relationships throughout the years and it increases in tension the degree to which the couple does not have shared values. Values translate as how they spend money.

Michelle is not quite sure how to use her wealth, but at the same time, not undermine her husband. She sees that if Josh is to stop working, it will free up time, but he will clearly lose his own sense of identity. Needless to say, this scenario does not interest him. But driving two-and-a-half hours every day to New Jersey is straining the relationship. He is coming home exhausted.

The challenge is how to enter a conversation where everybody has strong emotions. On one level, Michelle wants her husband not to work as much. On the other hand, if he becomes more dependent on her wealth, she will get frustrated with Josh over time.

As I raise the topic with a sense of ease, it allows the three of us to take out a bit of the tension and look with new eyes. I ask, "How do you imagine yourselves combining your financial futures?"

Josh says, "Well, in order to afford what we now have, I am certainly going to have to work more. This standard is higher than what I am accustomed to."

He says this in response to the fact that Michelle has recently purchased the house where they now live. Michelle says, "Well, as far as I am concerned, we need to think less about what you contribute, and more about what makes sense given how we want to live and the discrepancy in our incomes."

I can see that this step is going too fast. Josh has not yet considered how he can spend money from Michelle and feel good about it. As far as he is concerned, Michelle has a higher standard of living, which means he is going to need to work harder to afford it.

I ask if I can take a moment and set a broader context for the talk. I share my relationship with money. "I have seen money as a resource. It's a form of energy. It's an opportunity. And once someone possesses that energy and doesn't harness it through control, it tends to create tension and animosity. Let's step back for a moment. Instead of asking ourselves how much we can spend, I'd like to ask, 'What is it that we actually want?'"

I can see that taking the discussion away from who is paying for what creates a lot more breathing space. Josh shares, "I know that driving five days a week to New Jersey is wearing on the family. But I don't have an alternative."

Michelle says, "I know that you need to work, but it would be great if we could take four days instead. I'd like that we have quality time, especially with the baby."

He replies, "I don't know how to reconcile that, because that cost would mean that I wouldn't be able to contribute as much to the family. I'd be more dependent on your income. I know you'll have a problem if I lose my independence and become dependent on you. That's not going to work for either of us."

She says, "I am fine with that. I know the quality of life to the family will far outweigh the financial sacrifice I'd be making."

Josh looks with wonder. "This whole concept of money as a means is foreign to me. I have never lived that way. I've always seen money as the end."

I reply, "Yes, now you can decide how you want to live and see what needs to be arranged financially. As long as both of you agree, there is no issue. If something comes up, take it seriously. That will make sure that you stay connected in this area."

We then turn to practical things. The couple proceeds from having no clear way forward to agreeing to a joint account that will begin their financial journey together. As we work through the details, Josh feels resistance. He asks, "How do I stop feeling guilty when spending that money? What do I get to buy without asking? I don't want to need to go to Michelle to ask to buy something."

We use the resistance to further their common understanding. By asking what will work for him, he says, "I'd be happy to keep some money in my own account where I can spend it freely." The details are worked out and a vision is forming.

In the end there is a lot of laughter as they see the lightness that can be brought to a topic that previously felt so heavy.

In my work I have seen that money and sex are two taboo subjects that make even the most free-spirited person shrink. I sense that this is in response to the social stigma cast upon these two subjects. Our beliefs and conditioning around them are deep. Creating space even, no, *especially* when a topic is stigmatized is critical to allowing for peace to be found. It is what I have been promoting with the radical self-love exercise, embracing whatever the emotion is, regardless of the judgment I have of it.

Michelle and Josh live differently with money and each of them can learn from their partner. It is an opportunity to see the power in both ways of existing in the world.

CHAPTER 37

A Totally Unreliable Friend

(New York, New York)

The next afternoon, I leave Rhinebeck and head to New York City. I'll be meeting up with my friend, Anthony, who owns a successful media company.

I told Anthony about my book project early on. When he heard my story, he told me how incredible it was. He says, "Brother, whatever I can do to help you bring this to the world, just ask." He tells me he will run a full-length article on his website. He asks nothing in return.

The sincerity of his offer is overwhelming. I find it hard to receive assistance, and therefore love. In my mind there is always the thought, "People have more important things to do with their lives," or, "If they help, I don't want to be obligated in return."

But really, I'm just scared. I see that when I let my guard down, it is easy to get hurt.

One thing has become clear: Radical self-love is the key to unlocking the heart and inviting others to see it. If I am not able to receive love, I will block. Shut down. Lose connection with my emotions, and thereby my connection with others.

I arrive at Anthony's office in the early afternoon. Our session is that evening, so we have some time to settle in and talk. We have a close friendship and he is very open to my reflections. We've had contact over the past few months, and I have seen several patterns emerge.

The first is an exaggeratedly slow time to reply. When we email, he'll often say, "I'll get back to you next week." It is almost never next week, but rather three or four weeks later. I have no dependency on him, so it is never a problem. In fact, I very much appreciate that he takes care of himself.

Yet I see an unsustainable behavior. Once I see a behavior, I feel into the implications of what it may develop into over a lifetime. It dawns on me that if he is making the same promises to everyone in his life, then he will be overrun in no time.

He is so openhearted and wants to help so many. I can imagine how behind he must feel in life, always catching up with promises he made when he could not have estimated his capacity to actually deliver what he promised. And I can imagine the frustration people feel when they do have expectations. In our time together, he is perpetually catching up and apologizing before every call. I have the thought that, instead of teaching him, I'd like to show him the absurdity of it.

I say something I know will set him off: "Anthony, I am really frustrated with you. You are totally unreliable."

Sure enough, he is triggered. It is completely contrary to his self-identity. He immediately apologizes, "Man, I am so sorry that it's taken so long."

I laugh out loud. "I am messing with you. How do you see it as your responsibility to apologize to me? You are doing me the favor. When did I get to impose myself on your schedule? I am grateful for everything you are doing for me. But I am afraid I am reinforcing a pattern in your life. I'm just another person you owe, weighing on you so you can get back to peace."

He interrupts, "No, I love the article. There are just things that have come up in between."

I say, "What I'm pointing at is not the fact that things come up. It's how you deal with it so the world is not your problem. There is no reason you should need to apologize every time you call someone. That's my point."

He perks up with interest. "Yes, I see this in myself. What do you suggest?"

I say, "Well, you know how we began this discussion with me saying you're unreliable?"

"Yes, of course."

"I did that because I know you don't want to be seen as unreliable. I'd like to invite you to embrace that part of yourself. Can you say, 'I am unreliable, and it's fucking great'?"

"No, I can't say that," he replies. "I don't want to be that way."

I try again. "I know that, but give it a shot. 'I am totally unreliable, and it's fucking great.' Celebrate it with me. I don't want you to get stuck in the idea that you're in service to everybody and not yourself."

He repeats. "I am totally unreliable, and it's fucking great. I am totally unreliable and it's fucking great."

I ask, "How do you get out of the state of being perpetually behind? By celebrating that you are not reliable."

"I can feel it but it's still not easy for me to say." He repeats it a few more times and begins to laugh.

I ask, "How does being unreliable change how you will interact in the future?"

"Well, when I admit I am unreliable, in a strange paradoxical way, I become reliable."

"Yes, that's it," I say. "How will you speak with others when they expect something of you and you're not sure when you can deliver?"

He replies, "'I'd love to. But in general I am not particularly reliable when it comes to these things, so it may take some time. Is that okay?'"

We laugh again and he says, "How could it be that easy? How can I become reliable by saying to someone that I am unreliable?" In spite of the question, the logic is totally clear to him.

Then, he reveals, "Andy, there is one thing that is clear to me. I don't want to hurt people's feelings. What I am starting to see is that my desire not to hurt people's feelings is exactly the thing that does hurt them in the end. People are sensitive and they hear what you're not saying. They sense the feeling you're not expressing. And that makes them even more insecure and uncomfortable because they know you're not being fully frank with them."

As he speaks, it feels like he is channeling a deeper part of himself. As if he is speaking and listening to his own words and is surprised at how much they make sense.

I respond, "Your logic of not wanting to hurt a person is exactly the thing that hurts them."

"Yeah. But how can I do anything with that?"

I say, "Well, I can tell you what I do in my life. I follow a very simple rule. I ask myself, 'What's the scariest thing to admit?'" We've been discussing some issues he's having with his girlfriend. I say, "Consider your girlfriend, for example. What's the scariest thing to admit about that relationship?"

He ponders, then says, "The scariest thing is that when I tell her the truth, she will feel attacked."

"How about starting out conversations that way? 'I am worried I might hurt you, and that's not what I want to do. But

I'm not sure if we can work this relationship out.' That would be the open, honest, free way of interacting."

He asks, "So I would be authentic with what I'm feeling, instead of hiding my emotions and having them come out in twisted ways?"

I reply, "Yes. Let's try another one. How would it be for you if you felt comfortable enough to share your feelings, without necessarily seeing it as a problem, either for you or the other? You are not imposing your way, but rather sharing your feelings and allowing that to become a dialogue."

Anthony's face looks strained as he tries to grasp it. He continues to fall back on the insecurity of not wanting to hurt others. I ask, "Where does that hurt come from?"

He says, "Well, my father shouted a lot. I've never wanted to be like that."

"Can you give me an example?" I ask.

"When we went to the restaurant, if he wasn't happy, he'd shout at me at the top of his lungs in the middle of the restaurant. I remember being eight years old and I was deeply embarrassed. I tried to hide it, but it hurt. I have that image of my father— yelling at me—seared into my head. When I speak with others, I never want them to have that feeling I felt in that moment."

I ask, "What would be the most frightening thing to say right now?"

He says, "I am afraid that if I am truly myself, I'll turn into my dad."

I ask, "And how would that change things?"

He replies, "I'd get much quicker to the point. I wouldn't obfuscate, scared that I might hurt the person."

We have a big laugh at this relieving conclusion and finish our martinis. The waiter comes to our table and says, "The bar is closed. The drinks are on the house. Have a great night."

CHAPTER 38

Father Mahoney Talks, I Listen

(Charlottesville, Virginia)

I enter Charlottesville for the first time in my life, where I visit my friend Jeff. Two years earlier, when he was twenty-eight years old, Jeff came to me and asked for help. He was the head of a company, and was in over his head. The company had gone through several leadership changes over the years. Four over a two-year period, to be exact.

Back then, as he described the culture, it was apparent to me that it was toxic and he should have not taken the job. Over twenty years of dealing with organizational development, I had learned that some situations are bigger than our desire to do the right thing.

Given his lack of experience in addressing such a toxic work environment, I said, "Although I would love to help you, this project is too much trouble. I am afraid I'll have to decline."

He declared, "Andy, I am going to do this with or without you."

At that moment, I felt the full surrender. When I saw him stand in this certainty, I had two thoughts: *He's insane*, and, *He could use a friend on the journey he is about to undertake*.

"Okay, I guess we're going to do this," I consented.

He was immediately confused. "What changed?" he asked.

"You're going to need a friend." About a year later, he realized I did it because I loved him. I saw he was someone I would be willing to sit with in the struggle. Like two soldiers lying next to each other in a foxhole, seeing the bullets fly over their heads. We spent the next year struggling together as close friends.

In that year, he quit his job, asked his girlfriend to marry him, moved to a new state, married, and nine months later, had a baby. On top of all this, he re-entered school to study religion and law. How he will use these two disciplines together has yet to be decided. He is very tied to his religion and he has an intellectual curiosity, which leads to many interesting discussions between us. Although I'm not into faith, I am always open to anyone who values deep reflection.

When I arrive in Charlottesville, he invites me along for a meeting he has with one of his professors, Father Mahoney, a feisty Jesuit priest. I can see in Jeff's eyes that he relishes the idea of me sitting with a church "encyclopedia." I think he sees us as two unique chemical compounds that have never been tested together.

Father Mahoney lives in a nice tree-lined neighborhood. His front lawn is overgrown. As he opens the door, Jeff says to him, "I hope you don't mind that I brought a friend. He is on a book tour and I think he might appreciate being with us."

The father looks me up and down and reserves any comment. I am amused by his lack of hospitality, but I wasn't expected, so I do not have any expectations.

He is eighty-five years old. The way he talks, it seems like the older he gets, the more things he resents. He gripes, "Jesuit priests have no idea what they are doing today. They don't see that giving a eulogy has nothing to do with opinions. Their lack of academic background is frightening. How the church could move so far away from its roots is beyond me. Priests are getting more and more latitude to share the word in a way that suits them."

Jeff mentions a second time that I have written a book and the Father asks, "What's it about?"

I reply, "A dramatic experience I had as a child and how I healed from it."

He responds, "Were you molested by a priest?" He asks this with complete disregard for how painful it might be for someone who has experienced such trauma. I shake my head in the negative and he moves onto the next subject.

Books fill every inch of his house. There are pictures intermingled with some of them. It feels like I am looking at a representation of his brain. Father Mahoney is obviously into knowledge. It's also obvious that one does not come with him to discuss, but rather listen. He relishes an audience and he has what appears to be two willing listeners.

For the next two hours, he and Jeff discuss church doctrine. The father is able to recall the most minute details. At some point, I give up trying to understand. I spend most of my time tracking time. As in, *How much longer will we be here?*

As we drive back to his wife and newborn child, I ask Jeff, "What interests you so much about all this stuff?"

He explains, "Andy, when you're studying religious doctrine, it's not about what makes sense or doesn't make sense. It's about the implications of any single decision. If the church releases a new piece of a doctrine, it has implications for all the existing doctrine. It's like computer code. You can't change one line of it without it having implications for all the others."

Now my interest has perked up. "What's an example of that?"

He asserts, "Well, if the church were to ever accept that Jesus was not conceived immaculately, then the most obvious implication would be that Mary was not a virgin when she had Jesus. This would then have an implication that Jesus is fallible."

As he speaks, it dawns on me that, not unlike the church, we all have our own doctrines. We don't necessarily write them out, but we have them in our heads. The degree to which we combine all these doctrines, which are translated into beliefs, is a complex system of interconnected ideas. If any one of our beliefs is confronted, there are implications for so many others.

For instance, once I embraced the fact that my dad loved me, I had to let go of all the stories of what a terrible person he was. The grudge I had for so many years could not remain. Not unlike the church doctrine, my own mental doctrine could only be overhauled if I threw out the entire book.

CHAPTER 39

Stuck at Thomas Jefferson's Home

(Charlottesville, Virginia)

When I leave Jeff's home, I have about nine hours before I need to be at my next appointment in Virginia Beach. Since it's only about a three-hour drive, I have time to spend. Jeff mentions that Thomas Jefferson's home, Monticello, is on the way, so I decide to go there.

While I drive, a cold rain slices through cold air. The trees start to form icicles which look like chandeliers.

When I arrive, I walk to the admission counter to find out that the actual home is up a hill and I need to take a shuttle bus. We take the shuttle bus and the tour begins. As we walk through the home, I hear strange crackling sounds outside. We are not exactly sure what's making the sounds, but one of the guides says, "We are initiating the inclement weather protocol."

Apparently, the ice I was appreciating so much on my drive has now grown so heavy that many trees on the property are beginning to fall over, and some have already fallen over the entry road.

The tour is cut short and we are taken to the bottom floor, which is the kitchen quarters. I can see that our guide is not exactly sure what to do next. I ask, "Has this ever happened to you before?"

She replies, "Not in the fifteen years I've worked here."

No one can let us know when we can leave because there are so many fallen trees blocking traffic. I look at my watch and see that I have six hours to get to the next stop. Since it's a three-hour drive, I'm not particularly worried.

To wait out the storm, we are shuffled into a small break room that is used by the guides. Chairs are arranged in a circle. We sit and wait. An hour passes. A child in the group begins to have a panic attack as we sit in the windowless room. The guide brings her some chocolate in hopes that it might calm her. Although we have no specific reason to feel unsafe, there is a strange fear in the room.

Going into the second hour, the guide invites us to ask questions while we wait. There are a lot of questions, especially because the room we are in is filled with photos and the family tree of Thomas Jefferson's mistress. She was a fourteen-year-old slave at the time, and I faintly remember discussions around how this relationship was judged over the years.

It is clear that the guide has been taught how to engage the subject matter. In essence, they have been taught how to discuss the period without passing judgment. They are also prepared on how to address issues when they arise. I understand this when the guide shares, "We are not supposed to discuss our opinions on this matter."

But since we are stuck in the same room for such a long

period, she eventually relents and says, "I'm not supposed to discuss this, but I'll share my thoughts. Please understand that this is not part of the tour." There are no black people in the group and I don't believe she would feel comfortable to share if there were.

She continues, "It wasn't often discussed until more recent history. But after Thomas Jefferson's wife died, he took a slave as a mistress. This slave, Sally Hemings, was fourteen years old at the time. He had six children with her. When I tell this story, people often react aggressively. One time a woman shouted, 'It was not a relationship, she was raped! Tell the truth. She was raped!'"

She continues, "I believe the problem is that we have elevated Thomas Jefferson to almost god-like status. But he was human, just like any of us. So to elevate him is to disregard that he was also flawed. It would be easy for us to judge him from our context today, but that would be dismissing the context in which he lived. He inherited slaves and at the same time was against slavery. If Jefferson had released his inherited slaves, they would have had to travel to the North. They likely wouldn't have survived the trip."

I appreciate the wisdom and delicacy with which she approaches the subject. She sees both sides and doesn't have a strong opinion either way. Over my lifetime, I've slowly moved away from people with strong opinions. I have found that if I don't adopt their opinions, I am seen as part of the problem.

As I write this, I see the potential projections made upon me: "If he knew the real story, he would not be writing this way." Or even, "He is just ignorant." I contemplate leaving these sections out of the book for fear that it might alienate readers or even worse, generate animosity.

I have realized that everyone holds beliefs. I have little to no interest in people's beliefs. What I am intensely interested in, however, is what has caused them to create those beliefs. This is what brings us together in our shared humanity. Thomas

Jefferson is just an idea that elicits emotions. If I allow these emotions to go uninvestigated, I am lost. If I see these emotions as an opportunity to explore what makes me feel this way, space emerges and I see the world with clear and wonder-filled eyes.

I am certainly not a historian and I don't profess to understand the cultural dynamics of any period. What I have found to be true, though, is that when we sling labels at people, we are then no longer able to see them as individuals in our shared humanity. We can no longer understand the context in which someone lives, and we lose connection within ourselves and with them.

Once we make it personal by projecting an image onto them, we ourselves are locked into a belief. Everything we do needs to validate that point. And if there's one thing that has been lost in America, on all sides of the political divide, it is the ability to reflect on how one feels, and the knowledge that how one feels isn't necessarily a claim to truth. Rather, it is an opinion that can be held lightly in order to engage with others with differing opinions.

Jefferson is the quintessential person who can be seen in different lights. He wrote that all men are equal under the law, while at the same time he was owning slaves. It begs the question how such hypocrisy can exist. How we interpret that is what separates us. Some see it as a sign of the times, while others see it as willful neglect. Both sides are correct in their assertions, and at the same time incorrect. Each side decides the context they find relevant when making the argument.

When we start judging before we consider the context, we are left with two competing beliefs. This can only end in name-calling and mudslinging.

As the guide continues, I glance at my watch. If I don't leave in the next forty-five minutes, I will be late for the next session in Virginia Beach. I begin to fear that my window of opportunity might close if I don't do something soon. "I have a bit of a predicament," I tell the guide. "If possible, I'll need to find a way to get off the mountain sooner."

"Is it an emergency?" she asks.

I reply, "Well, I am supposed to be at an event where I will be speaking about my book."

"Are you an author?" she asks.

I laugh inside as I think how long I have come to accept that I'm an author. Now I am forced to proclaim it in order to get off the mountain. "Yes, I am an author," I say.

She hesitates as if she is sizing me up. Then she grabs her walkie-talkie and says to it, "We have an author who needs to get to a book signing. We need to find a way to get him to the parking lot."

I feel people in the group looking at me as if they might be sitting next to someone famous. Little do they know that I have only sold a few hundred copies of my book.

The guide receives a response on the walkie-talkie. I'm escorted to a woman named Judy, who will help me get to my car. Her first question is, "Are you the author?"

"Yes," I say.

She walks me to the front door, which has turned into a staging area to evacuate groups. She hands me off to the next guide who asks, "Are you the author?"

Again, I reply, "Yes, I am the author."

I am treated with surprising grace as I wait. Apparently, everyone with a walkie-talkie is aware of my status. They take it as a shared mission to get the author off the mountain. It is an amazing moment for me as I feel how beautiful it is to surrender to full self-acceptance.

I wait on the front porch. There, two of the guides are waiting and preparing for the shuttles. One says, "So, you're the author."

"Yes, that's me," I reply once again.

Eventually a shuttle arrives and I'm driven to my car. I see the freshly-cut trees that have been removed from the road. As I sit in my car, I am flooded with gratitude. I cry at the display of love and care I have received. There is nothing more beautiful in life than surrendering to the acceptance of love. I have spent so many years pushing it away in different ways, and to have it handed to me in such abundance is overwhelming.

To the people of the Jefferson Museum, thank you for the love you showed me. You'll never know how a simple act of caring supported me, not only in getting off the mountain in time, but seeing that I could embrace love. Especially for something I was struggling with: *I am an author, and it's fucking great.*

CHAPTER 40

Finding Forgiveness

(Virginia Beach, Virginia)

I quickly make my way off the mountain and away from the ice storm. It's a rainy drive and I look at the time regularly. My next stop is my publisher John's house. I asked John three weeks ago if he would like to host a session. He replied, "I am not sure people in my network would like to join a book launch event."

I explained, "It's not a book launch, rather a letter-writing exercise." While I explained it, I could hear something in his voice change. It was as if he finally understood the journey I was on.

He left the conversation saying, "Let's see if we can make this happen." He has followed through.

I make it to John's office a few minutes before the group arrives for the session. When we're ready to start, there are six of us around the table. It's an interesting session because all the attendees are authors in their own right. Each one of us has had some dramatic experience in our lives and have used that pain to serve others.

We go around the room and everyone shares what they do. I'm most touched by the story of Regina, a woman who appears to be in her sixties. She has a strong presence, like an actress. She shares that she was abused as a child, and she has created a program to support victims of child abuse. She developed a marionette doll named Simon Says. She takes her marionette to classrooms throughout the US and uses it as a tool to heighten awareness around sexual abuse.

Throughout the performances she gives, the children will often react and it becomes apparent which ones are suffering from abuse. I feel my stomach drop. How scary it is to feel that any one of her performances might actually lead to an arrest. And, as she explains, they often do. Counselors and police are onsite, ready to support the kids on the spot. Regina shares that more than 200 predators have been caught as a result of the program.

It's incredible to be with someone who has taken the greatest pain in her life and transferred it into something greater than herself. I am not alone on my journey. There is something magical about transforming one's pain into something wondrous. Like a caterpillar that spins a cocoon, and emerges as a butterfly.

When we come to the letter-writing portion of the session, Regina asks me, "Who would you suggest we write?"

I reply, "I cannot speak for you. I can only say that I often ask myself whom I most resist writing to. And whoever pops up, I write to them."

I see her body contract at the thought. Her eyes tear up. "I don't think I can write to him."

I share, "You certainly don't need to write to this person.

Allow yourself to write to whomever feels right for you at this moment."

I do not want her to feel pushed. I can see her feelings run deep. I've learned that pushing people when they are feeling intense emotions can re-traumatize, and then it's hard to feel safe. Once a space has been created to revisit old emotions, I have learned how important it is to let people take baby steps. Any hint of forcing emotions will often create a defensive response.

With that, the writing begins. As she writes, tears stream down her face. She is touching a deep pain. She finishes and puts the letter face-down.

I invite people to share their letters. Regina shares, "When I was a child, I was abducted by a man and raped and tortured for days. I eventually escaped. I was beaten so badly that I would have died if I had not been found by a passerby. The torment of that experience was so deep that I have never considered writing my abductor, or moreover, forgiving him."

Regina does not read her letter, but shares some basic details. It is a beautiful moment and we are all touched by her grace and forgiveness. Several people have tears in their eyes. We share for about an hour and a half, cherishing the pain that has brought us together. We barely know each other and yet we are closer than any of us could have imagined.

After leaving the session, I start feeling cracks in the "and it's fucking great" self-acceptance practice. When people are in touch with their emotions, all we can do is sit with them in their suffering. This is not easy to do because it often means allowing uncomfortable feelings. So instead of just companioning people in pain, we try to fix them. And usually, this comes down to us trying to get rid of the uncomfortable feelings we have in ourselves, versus being purely motivated by a genuine concern for the other person.

When we are totally at peace with our own suffering, then

holding that same space for another is easy. I see that the degree to which a person has made peace with their own suffering is the degree to which they can be a "wounded healer" to others.

I have learned through the "and it's fucking great" practice that when people are unable or unwilling to go to into the pain that underlies their thoughts, those thoughts repeat like a broken record. They never release. When we're not pushing pain away, it begins to settle in our system. And in time, the pain begins to be loved. The goal of this tool is not to create a release or spiritual awakening. It is about short-circuiting our desire to move away from pain, and by doing that, allowing us to experience the world in a new light.

In my own life, I use formal methods and tools lightly so that they help create awareness, without limiting myself to them. The moment we adopt a tool, we must also be aware that it will come with its own limits. In the case of the "it's fucking great" tool, I am experiencing the limits of embracing the thing that's hardest to acknowledge. In this moment, it is not about embracing it, but simply giving it a place, which is different.

Imagine if, when Regina told me her story, I had said, "You were abducted and raped and it's fucking great." My stomach drops at the thought. When she shared her experience and letter, she was fully in touch with her emotion. She was allowing the pain and not trying to solve it in any way. There was no need for the "it's fucking great" practice.

I am beginning to count down the days until my final destination, which gives me time to reflect. Regina has brought my awareness to something I have not fully considered on my journey until now: forgiveness. When Regina shared her letter, it dawned on me that I, too, have a letter I have not yet written.

CHAPTER 41

Transcending Forgiveness

(Savannah, Georgia)

*W*hile in Georgia, I get an email from an old high school friend, whom I have not seen or spoken with in years, which reads, "Hey, have you had any contact with the woman who killed your mother?"

I am both surprised and confused. I haven't given her much thought since my mom's death. I don't feel any resentment, nor do I have any unresolved feelings about the experience. I think, *Why would I write her?* But the question stays with me, which then leads me to think, *What do I have to say to her?*

It dawns on me that I have never considered what she has gone through. She may have never recovered from the accident. It hits me that two people died that evening thirty years ago: my mother and this woman's innocence. She lost whatever sense of a carefree life she might have had. Whatever caused her to drink so much that night, it may very well have been the only thing she could do to numb her pain.

For years, I was very much focused on my own pain. I couldn't create space for anyone else's baggage because carrying my own was already enough. Now I feel compelled to write to her. I want to share my love and forgiveness and let her know that she does not need to live in torment.

I ponder on forgiveness as I drive to my next session in Orlando. I struggle with the concept. The challenge I see is that, in order for me to forgive, I need to make the assumption that the other is, in some way, guilty to begin with.

In my heart, there is something missing in this way of thinking. It misses the point that people behave in ways they wish they wouldn't. It is missing compassion. We all make mistakes. How is the woman responsible for my mother's death just a reflection of me? If I assume someone is wrong and I am right, where is the compassion? It feels like I am managing my emotions through blame. If someone who hurts me is "bad," then I have someone to blame for my suffering. But what if there was no one to blame?

My thoughts turn to the difference between self-acceptance, allowing an emotion to settle, and self-love, which is embracing it completely. My feeling is that forgiveness, in the traditional sense, falls into the grouping of self-acceptance. I will give this emotion a place so that it no longer haunts me. In my struggle to fully love myself, I ask myself what reality I want to live in. Do I want to be a person who loves partially and selectively, or universally and unconditionally? Or am I someone who loves conditionally?

I no longer desire to live in the world of traditional forgiveness and self-acceptance. At the moment, I am inspired by love.

Instead of me forgiving the other, I want to forgive myself for not being able to love. I love the fact that I am not always able to love.

l see my struggle to love fully most pronounced in the relationship with my father. I spent years trying to forgive him for how he treated me. The years of trying to manage these emotions got me nowhere. The closer I think I got to forgiving him, the more disconnected I felt inside. I was rationally constructing a way to say, "The past is the past." But I was living the tension every day.

Then I had an epiphany. My father did everything he did because he loved me. Of course, at times his behavior was abhorrent, but it was done because of his incapacity to feel his own emotion. What if I took all of the things I had judged in him, and accepted that they were just examples of his love for me? Instead of forgiving him, I'd have to forgive myself for not seeing it all those years.

I did not "forgive" my father. Rather, I overcame the limited idea of thinking that he needed to be forgiven in the first place. Now, instead of asking myself if I have forgiven someone, I ask myself what is it that I am having trouble loving. It's almost always the case that whatever I have trouble loving in the other, I have trouble loving in myself.

I don't see people as good or bad, right or wrong. I see good people who make mistakes. That does not mean they shouldn't be held accountable for their mistakes. It just means that I do not need to get stuck in judgment. I don't need to get lost in thoughts from the past that bring me nowhere but feeling emotionally disconnected. Their behavior is no longer my problem.

It took me time to actually see my father and the woman who killed my mother through my own pain. For years, I only saw them at their worst moments, in the parts that were easy to blame. All it did for me was to rerun my stories of anger and blame, over and over.

With these thoughts on my mind, during my next session I write the following letter to the woman who killed my mother:

> *Dear Sheryl,*
>
> *I am not even sure what I want to write. On one hand, I am helpless to share my anger, as it is masked in years of pain. In this single act, you took away the one thing that made my life worth living. In this loss, my entire life was turned upside down.*
>
> *It is only more recently that I have begun to feel the beauty of this loss. The beauty of remembering the mother that I loved. The mother that made me feel safe.*
>
> *I now see that you clearly had a life very different than my own. I can't imagine what led you to drink so much that evening, or how you live with the guilt that you must have had all of these years. I cannot imagine how that would feel.*
>
> *I do not know if you are alive or if you have since passed on. I would want you to know that I have deep compassion for your loss. In that single moment, you lost part of your future. You lost the opportunity to go through life anonymously. You had an unfortunate label that no jail sentence could take away.*
>
> *I have told you before and I tell you again, you are forgiven. You need not live in shame or guilt. Life's too short and I would hate for two lives to have been lost in this tragedy.*
>
> *I love you. I always have. If I see you in the future, I will put both my arms around you and hug you until you feel the love that was always meant for you.*
>
> *Our lives have been brought together through fate. We have a connection that will never change. I'd like to cherish you for the person who was never fully seen. I*

am very sorry that you had to hold that tension. It is now time for us both to heal. You are always welcome in my life.

Love,

Andy

CHAPTER 42

Thrown Out of the House

(Orlando, Florida)

In the evening, I arrive at the home of my friend, Susan, in Orlando. I am met by her, her husband Vincent, and their daughter. I immediately sense something is off. Vincent sizes me up with such an aggressive energy that I ask Susan if there is something we can do to make him feel more comfortable.

The aggression builds over time. On our second night together, I share some of my discoveries. I say, "I see that there are two drivers for any action. Either avoiding pain or seeking pleasure."

He says, "That's not true. All the books say that."

I ask, "I am not a big reader. What books do you mean?"

"All books," he replies.

I ask, "What's an alternative?"

He responds, "You can do nothing."

I think, and then respond, "I guess so, but would that also be because one was avoiding pain or seeking pleasure?"

He stutters. I can see he is not looking to have a dialogue but instead is trying to make a point. Trying to put me in my place. I am not particularly interested in winning an argument, which gives him little to argue with. Clearly, his identity is tied to feeling a sense of superiority.

I have worked with Susan for years and she never mentioned this aspect of her life. It is all starting to make sense. There are things I have been unaware of all of these years. The aggression grows. A passive aggressive comment here. A door slamming there. It materializes to be far more overtly aggressive, even verging on physical. I ask what we can do to ease whatever stress I may be causing by being in the house. Susan tells me not to worry about it. Apparently, this is normal behavior.

My work with Susan is to help her find her own voice. To stand strong and to be clearer in her needs. She is the head of a nonprofit organization that supports victims of sex trafficking. Although I think I am helping her transition to the next phase of her company's development, what I am actually doing is giving her a voice. And I am unaware that this voice is so threatening to her husband. This all comes to a head on the last night, at the dinner table.

His aggression has escalated and he says, "When are you going to stop with the handouts? When are you going to give her some real money? You're treating her like she is nothing."

I am confused because her nonprofit has received over a million dollars. Apparently, he believes more is required. I sit dumbfounded, wondering if he has had too much to drink. I've never been in a situation where I was volunteering my time to help someone build, and then been verbally assaulted. In spite of this, I realize he is looking out for his wife's interests, no matter how ill-conceived his approach might be.

He huffs away from the table. I share, "I'd love to see more money come into the company. But the main investor won't do so if he feels that there is incompetence in areas."

In this moment, you can cut the air with a knife. He walks over to me while I have food in my mouth and says, "Don't call my wife incompetent. Not in my house. You called my wife incompetent."

I swallow and say, "I did not say your wife is incompetent. I said that the main investor would not put more money in if he felt he was funding incompetence."

Susan and I look at one another with confusion, not sure if he is just kidding. It is so far away from the discussion that we were having that his reaction makes no sense.

Susan interjects, "Honey, you don't understand. It's not what he said. You're not hearing him."

He only gets more aggressive. "No, you don't understand," he barks.

I try again, "I am not sure you understand what I was saying."

He interrupts, standing above me. "I understand exactly what you are saying. You said my wife is incompetent. Not in my house. Apologize now."

His eyes are filled with rage. I know this rage from my childhood. But I no longer live in fear of it. I see it for what it is: a deep inability to feel one's pain. I can see he is hoping to start a fight. Susan looks at me with eyes of fear, not sure if I'll defend myself.

He continues to shout, "Apologize to my wife!"

I quietly look at him and shake my head in disappointment. I've learned not to engage someone who is charged with that level of aggression. There is no interacting. It's just about moving away from the threat. I get up from the table, pack my bag, and leave.

On the way out, I thank Susan for the time together. I say, "Please do not worry about it. Or me. I'll be fine."

It is interesting because the situation is so counter to the love and connection I've been overwhelmed by on my journey.

The next day, Susan and I meet up. She tells me she also left the house last night and slept somewhere else. She shares, "Over the years, I have given up more and more to make peace with him. I gave up my own strength to keep the peace. I separated from my family. I separated from my friends. I even stopped bringing business associates around for fear of how he might behave. After years of trying to keep the peace, I have slowly moved away from the people in my life who might trigger him. I have done my best to manage it."

I have a beautiful moment as I realize that it is my ability to hold space that gives her the opportunity to reflect on her life and how she wants to move forward.

I am very much open to supporting her in her struggle. What I do not want is to validate the reality that keeps her unaware of her husband. It's safe to assume that Vincent had an emotional trauma as a child, and that's how Susan justifies his behavior. I have seen that, on face value, this would appear loving. Showing understanding for someone else's struggle. But the reverse side of this is that it enables more of the same behavior. As the person does not want to draw a hard boundary, the behavior is allowed to continue. Just as Vincent did not have a boundary, neither did Susan.

I was aware when I left the table that there was little chance Susan and I would speak much going forward. I knew that in order for her to comfortably go back to Vincent, she would need to normalize their behavior. And the only way that was going to happen was for her to defend his actions.

Sure enough, two days later I get an email from Susan that breaks my heart. She has gone from understanding how her husband's behavior has impacted her life for years to articulating a written explanation of how his actions are warranted. I am saddened, but not surprised. I've learned that when it comes to working through problems, it's easiest to pick the narrative that suits the outcome we're looking to achieve.

I respond and let her know that I will not be able to work on her project any longer. I'm not going to place anyone in the uncomfortable situation where we may be in the middle of a discussion and her husband might enter. It is a beautiful moment for me because I get the opportunity just to say, "No." Accommodating any form of abuse or aggression is not something I need to make time for, regardless how much suffering he might be going through.

The irony is that in trying to push me away and protect his wife, Vincent has upset her life and sabotaged her business, and in doing so, has made her more dependent on him. In the name of protecting her, he has made her life less secure. He will never see it that way because he will of course say, "I did it to protect her."

What stands out to me is how we, through our best intentions, allow people to abuse us. Every reaction in life can be justified. We can explain why we lashed out at someone and even make it out to be their fault. We have no choice in how others decide to justify their actions.

What we do have is the opportunity to hold people accountable. In not doing so, we are perpetuating the same thing we want to see change. Learning how to set boundaries is challenging for most people because it can carry serious consequences. In this case, it has the potential to lead to divorce.

This all comes back to a theme I have seen often: fear. Once fear sets in, what we are willing and able to look at is severely compromised. The only way out of this vicious cycle is to either embrace what I want, or reject what I don't want. Either way, it all comes back to self-love.

The first step is to accept reality as it is. In Susan's case, "I am in a relationship with a dominating man who is incapable of managing his emotions, and it's great." If she were to judge him, she would automatically become a victim of his incapacity. By not judging him, but simply accepting him as he is, she remains empowered to choose.

By loving where we are, we can not only establish boundaries around what we don't want, but also create a vision of where we really want to be. Self-love allows us to create a new world, not based in a reaction to a negative, but a calling to a positive.

CHAPTER 43
Give What You Want to Receive

(Fort Lauderdale, Florida)

*I*t is Thanksgiving and my friend Luke, who lives in Fort Lauderdale, is visiting his parents for the holidays. Luke studied at Harvard and has a brilliant mind. We have been in contact over the past few years, and I decide to deviate from my path to see him.

When I arrive and sit at the table with his parents, I can see something is off. The strong, intelligent man I knew is not sitting at the table with me. It dawns on me that although Luke is in his forties, he is sitting at the table with his parents, which means I am with a younger, more tender version of him.

It never ceases to amaze me how we often regress to a younger self when we are with our parents or other family. Our unresolved emotions come up and we go right back to our childhood selves, only in a larger body. I know it of course from my own life, so it is not a big surprise. Yet I only know Luke from our interactions together, so seeing him with his parents takes me a minute to recalibrate.

I can see Luke has a hard time being with his emotions now. His face is strained. At the table, I laugh and make light of the situation. "So what are we going to talk about?"

He replies, "We can talk about anything."

I don't want to make him feel more uncomfortable, so I say, "We can do that, or we can go out to the dock and enjoy the view."

He takes the opportunity for us to spend some time alone. We sit on the dock facing the beautiful bay.

Luke shares, "I have difficulty interacting with my parents. It always feels forced. I don't feel seen when I speak."

I ask, "How have you dealt with it?"

He says, "Well, they haven't been the parents I wanted them to be. And I tend to move away from them to cope."

I share, "I guess that is to be expected if you share with somebody and you don't feel you're getting what you need in return. What it is you want from them? What are they not giving you?"

He replies, "When I share what I am doing they have a way of diminishing it, as if there is something more I could be doing. Something that's more in line with their idea of success."

As he speaks, I think back on the past few months. The one lesson I've learned is that unconditional love has the power to heal more than words. I feel a sensation come over me and, without saying a word, I stand up and hug him on the dock. I give him love. Unconditional love, without judgment or need for anything in return.

In the past months, I've seen clearly that if you don't meet people where they are, they will likely flee. I sense that if I give people the slightest thing to react to, they'll use that to move away from their discomfort.

As I hug him I ask, "How does it feel to be loved?"

He smiles back. "Good."

I ask, "How would it feel if you just gave them that love and allowed them to feel the sensation?"

I can see the disdain come back over him. "But they would push it away."

"What if that was okay?" I ask.

He takes a deep breath.

I say, "I'd love to try something with you. How would it be if you said, 'My parents aren't really interested in what I am doing, and it's great. They have never given me what I need, and it's fucking wonderful.'"

He sits for a moment, then smiles. He repeats it a few times, each time with a bigger grin.

I ask, "Can you imagine loving them even more for not being there for you emotionally?"

He replies, "That would be great."

"Now let's go back to how it would feel when your dad says, 'I am not interested in your courses.' What would you say to him?"

"I'd say something like, 'I can imagine that. I probably wouldn't be interested either, if I were you,'" he says, laughing.

I ask, "How would it be if you met him in complete love, regardless of what he had to say? No resistance. How would that change your life?"

I can see the twinkle in his eye as he contemplates it. "But how do I get my head around the fact that I feel a certain way? I feel anger."

I reply, "Yeah, of course you may feel a certain resistance. You may even feel anger. But the more you allow that anger to define you, and believe it's your parents' fault, the more you're going to be pushing them away. And that's the irony. The degree to which you need them is the degree to which you hold them responsible for how you feel. It's not their responsibility. It's yours.

"If you want to receive love, you have to learn to give it unconditionally, without expectation, just as you desire it from them."

He smiles as if he is caught and has no other option.

I continue, "When you hug them, you are actually hugging the parts of you that need it. At the same time, you're hugging the child in your parents who also hasn't been able to feel their emotion. You are breaking the cycle."

He responds, "I can't do that yet. I need to be in a position of strength. I would feel weak, and I have always been the weak son. I don't want to be that any longer."

I say, "I see that, but it is your decision to see it as weakness. You hug them not from weakness, but from strength. Not because you need it. Because you all need it."

He nods. "I see that."

"So what you see as the problem, as weakness, could potentially change everything. And at the same time, let's acknowledge what happens when you don't hug. You're withholding something you desire, which could bring all of you together.

"Stated otherwise, be grateful that they are exactly who they are. They are perfect. You'll find that whoever you think they are will shift once you give them unconditional love."

He asks, "Can we go to a concrete example? My mother is always anxious. She is so fearful that I live in California that she constantly reminds me of the earthquakes and the violence. She tells me everything that can go wrong."

"And how does that make you feel?"

"Terrible."

"Why? She's only expressing her love for you."

"But it's annoying," he replies.

I ask, "What if you embraced it for what it really is? Her love for you. What if you showed appreciation for her concern? Every time she falls into her fear, you hug her and say, 'I know you're scared. It's going to be okay.' What if you used the opportunity to embrace what she is actually saying? That she is scared she is going to lose you. How beautiful is that?"

"I get it," he replies.

He walks me to my car and I open the trunk, sign the book for his parents, and give him some moonshine I brought with me from Virginia. We hug one last time and I jump back on the road. I drive an hour south to meet my mom's sister, Sue, and spend Thanksgiving with her, and with my brother who has flown in from Washington DC.

My journey will end in three days, and I'm ready to be home with Rani.

CHAPTER 44

Coming Home

(Miami, Florida)

I wake up on the second to last day before my return home to Amsterdam. My cousin's wife, Shauna, has arranged a session at a retirement community near Miami. I want to end at a retirement home because I feel these are the people who will best understand and appreciate my journey. The longer I live— the older I get—the more I cherish time.

About fifteen seniors show up to the session, ranging from eighty to over a hundred years old. The urgency I've been trying to share on this trip is now right in front of me. Before coming to the session, Shauna shared with me, with tears in her eyes, "In the last four years, I have lost 150 people. I knew each one of them."

I look around the room and am humbled. I cannot even begin

to imagine their life experiences. I have spent the past months feeling into the preciousness of every moment as I wrote Last Letters over and over again. And now it is the last time. Sixty sessions in three months, and this is the last.

I begin the session by sharing the journey and what it has meant to me. I cry. A lot. I have a mirror of understanding looking back at me, and all I can do is weep. I share what I've learned about love, compassion, and service to something greater than myself. I see the eyes of wisdom looking back at me. I share how the past three months have reshaped me with a depth of humility. I share how pain has guided me, and thereby, acted as a lighthouse for others. I share that I ran away from my pain and now, thirty years later, I've come back to its origins to live out what I couldn't then.

In both obvious and subtle ways, I spent years managing my sadness. But for the last few months, it has been my guide. I could never have imagined that inviting others to join me would be met with such warmth and kindness. Each person I have touched has touched me in return.

It is time for gratitude. It is received wholeheartedly by my current audience. When we break out to write letters, it is clear that many have not written in years. Their hands move slowly and methodically over the page. As we come back together, I ask if anyone would like to share who they wrote to, or even read the letter.

They aren't shy. Many of them wrote their parents. It is an amazing sight to see a ninety-year-old share the depth of her gratitude for her parents, and the depth of her sorrow at losing them. I can see that I still have the expectation that, at some point, I'll get over losing my mother. Hearing the words written to the parents of these people, it is clear that will never be the case. No matter how old I get, I'll always miss her. In many ways, I've spent the last months preparing others for that loss.

After the session, I get into my car and input the final destination: Miami International Airport. I feel a strange calm come over me. It almost feels numb. I could never have imagined this moment. I feel no sense that I've left things unsaid or undone. It feels like a dream I will wake from. It's all just a memory now. It feels confusing to think I'll be flying home today, instead of driving to another state for another session. I can just sit in the Miami sun and take it all in.

I am wondering if I'll experience an emotional crash at some point. I feel that crying over and over again in the sessions actually released any pent-up emotions I might have been feeling. But I don't know. I have always felt that allowing my emotions gave me more energy, not less. In the past I felt a tension that would build up. I would suppress my emotions and feel a buildup over time. But over the past three months, each session was its own emotional release.

At this moment, I just feel a deep sense of appreciation and gratitude. There were no major accidents. No major disruptions. I didn't miss a session. I didn't get lost. There was nothing dramatic. The only thing that I can think of where I felt any discomfort was when Vincent yelled at me at the dinner table. And even that wasn't that uncomfortable because it turned into a nice story.

I drive side streets to the airport looking for a post office where I can mail all the letters I've written over the past months. Sure enough, I find a space and park there. Feeling reflective, I thumb through the letters. I sort between those I've written to myself, to emotions, or to other people. I feel happy as I look down at all the letters, knowing they will soon be received by those I wrote to. I know I was full of love as I wrote them, so I trust they will be met with the intention they are sent.

I'm remembering the process I went through each time I wrote a letter. For the first few weeks, it was easy. I had a list of people for whom I feel grateful. Some of them were sitting in front of me as I wrote. But over time, it got harder. I would think, *Who will I write next?* But thinking hijacked the experience. By thinking, I was looking into the future and wondering how the letters might be received. I lost connection in this process.

So I started taking my own advice each time I wrote a letter: *I am going to fuck this up, and it's fucking great.* I would feel a sense of freedom come over me when I released the expectation to write an amazing letter.

After a while, I stopped deciding who to write before beginning. I resisted the urge to plan or think about it. I would let my hand decide. If I felt a wince of resistance, I asked myself, *What are you most afraid of at this moment?* This question centered me immediately and my hand would catapult into action.

I chose this question, as opposed to something like, "What are you grateful for?" It pulled me immediately into vulnerability. I couldn't answer this question without showing parts of myself that are challenging. Places where shame hides. Things I am suppressing. Fear of death, fear of exhaustion, fear of failing. Paradoxically, I lightened my load as I embraced each of these things inside of myself.

There were some wonderful surprises. In Lincoln, Nebraska, I wrote to the first person to hire me when I was just thirteen years old. I was struck by the trust she put in me at a young age. A letter gave me an opportunity to give her an unexpected gift. A chance to receive gratitude for just being herself, giving a young boy the chance to build up his self-confidence.

What I recognize in my own life is that people question their contribution to the world, especially those who have not done things that society might judge as remarkable. Yet what's truly remarkable are all the little acts of kindness that can easily go unseen. The things that are not done to get credit, but to support and love unconditionally.

In writing my letters, I saw that there have been many people in my life who touched me in ways they would quite possibly never know. My letter-writing was an opportunity to reach out to many of those people and let them know how they impacted my life. It was a time to love, and I cannot imagine anything more beautiful I could give these people.

As I drop the letters into the mail slot, I feel a deep sense of release. I did it. It is a moment of celebration. I committed to writing a letter any time I asked anyone else to do it. I am healing others as I am healing myself. Now those who were part of my journey, without even knowing it, will receive their letters. By dropping these letters into this box, I feel as if I have ended a chapter in my life. A symbolic gesture. A ceremony of surrender.

Yes, I am a wounded healer and pain is my greatest teacher. To the thousands of people who shared in this journey, I say, "I love you. Truly. Your willingness to join me will never be forgotten."

Lightning Source UK Ltd.
Milton Keynes UK
UKHW011941210720
366928UK00001B/31